THE COMPLETE
CANVASWORKER'S GUIDE

How to Outfit Your Boat Using Natural or Synthetic Cloth

Jim Grant

Illustrated and designed by Allan White

INTERNATIONAL MARINE PUBLISHING COMPANY
Camden, Maine

© 1985 by International Marine Publishing Company

Printed and bound by BookCrafters, Inc., Chelsea, Michigan

Published by International Marine Publishing Company
21 Elm Street, Camden, Maine 04843
(207) 236-4342

Library of Congress Cataloging in Publication Data

Grant, Jim (Jim Lowell)
    The complete canvasworker's guide.

    1. Marine canvas work.   I. Title.
VM531.G68 1985   623.8'62   85-14350
ISBN 0-87742-205-2

Publisher's Preface   iv
1   The Principles of Canvaswork   1
2   Awnings and Enclosures   15
3   Boat Covers   25
4   Bosun's Chairs   37
5   Cushions and Cushion Covers   45
6   Sail Covers   53
7   Small Covers   67
8   Companionway Dodgers and Bimini Tops   81
9   Flags and Pennants   99
10   Harnesses   109
11   Sail and Ditty Bags   119
12   Tote Bags   139
13   Sea Anchors   145
14   Weather Cloths and Hatch Covers   153
15   Windcatchers   161
      Appendix   172

Contents

We are pleased to offer this new edition of a tested and proven guide to the working of canvas. Under the title of *The New Canvas Worker's Library,* earlier editions have been used successfully by thousands of boat owners throughout North America, so we know that the instructions given herein provide an efficient and enjoyable means to the end: handsome, functional, and inexpensive canvas gear. It is time this book, which was published privately in the past, be given the broader distribution it deserves.

Jim Grant is unusual in that he is both an author and the owner of a mail-order company providing tools and materials for sailmakers and canvasworkers. Recognizing that those of us embarked on do-it-yourself projects are too often frustrated by the lack of a local outlet for needed supplies, we have included an Appendix listing some of the canvaswork necessities that Sailrite Kits makes available.

Enjoy your canvaswork.

Publisher's Preface

1

The
Principles
of
Canvaswork

The Principles of Canvas Work

This book is designed to acquaint you with the information which you will need to make all of the handy fabric items used by boaters. Fabric is particularly appropriate in the boating environment, because it can be made windproof, waterproof, flexible, strong, extremely durable, colorful, and easily repairable. Considering all these characteristics, fabric is also remarkably inexpensive.

FABRIC

But the word "fabric" is much too broad. Which fabrics are we talking about when we consider the boater's needs? The title of the section suggests that canvas will be our subject. The word "canvas," however, applies only if it is broadly defined as a tightly woven heavy-duty material. Forget that canvas always used to be made of hemp, flax, jute, or cotton. Today it is far more common to find boating canvas woven of synthetic fibers: acrylic, polyester, or nylon.

The use of synthetic materials in the production of canvas has led to a strength and durability which would have been inconceivable two decades ago. But there are still some who prefer the old natural fiber canvas. The reason is quite simple. The natural fibers swell when they get wet, further tightening the already tight weave and making them completely waterproof. Yet, as they dry, the fibers again return to normal size which permits the cloth to breathe and prevents condensation. Synthetic fibers do not swell — at least not very much. As a result, they can be made waterproof only by receiving a coating of vinyl or resin to close the cloth pores permanently. When condensation is unacceptable, as it is in all cover applications, synthetic canvases are treated with a water repellent finish which makes them "water resistant." When new, these repellent-treated fabrics are just as effective as the old natural canvases — they keep out water while nevertheless permitting the passage of enough air to prevent condensation. The trouble is that the water repellent finish tends to wear off and must be restored through a proofing spray. This is required every one to three years depending upon the use to which the fabric is put.

Thus some well-known boating authorities (Donald Street is one who comes to mind immediately) still recommend natural fiber canvas with a Vivatex or a similar type treatment. These treatments (also sold under the tradenames Graniteville, Terrasol, and Permasol among others) reduce the natural fiber's susceptibility to rot and mildew. Even so, my experience leads me to recommend the synthetic canvas over treated canvas. The latter will not last even a third as long as a good synthetic fiber canvas, and the synthetics are only slightly more expensive than the natural fiber canvas.

As I mentioned above, there are three synthetic fibers in current use: acrylic*, polyester*, and nylon. Each one has distinctive characteristics which must be understood if the best choice for a particular product is to be made.

Acrylic

Acrylic fibers are extremely resistant to rot from sunlight and smog. They also accept dye readily and resist fading better than any other outdoor fabric. There are two distinct methods of dyeing acrylic fabrics: (1) they can be "yarn dyed" prior to weaving and (2) they can be "vat dyed" after weaving. The first of these techniques is greatly superior to the second, although it is more expensive and reduces the choice of color patterns available (all color changes must parallel either the warp or the fill threadlines). Acrylan is available only in a "water resistant" finish which, of course, enables it to breathe sufficiently to eliminate condensation.

Unfortunately, Acrylan has one serious shortcoming. It is highly susceptible to damage from chafe. Thus, when using acrylic materials, be very careful to protect them at all wear points with leather or Dacron patches.

Polyester

Polyester fibers are nearly as resistant to sunlight as the acrylic ones, and they are stronger and more resistant to stretch. But they are not easily dyed, and the dye is not so colorfast as it is with acrylic fibers. Thus, for cover purposes, polyester is generally an economy choice—it does cost a bit less. Polyester is available in a vinyl-coated waterproof finish *(The best known trademark is "Weblon," but many other makes are available)* and in a water-resistant finish which breathes, called spun dacron (the tradename is Destiny 2 + 2). Standard Dacron sailcloth can be used for covers, but it is not very soft and it is not treated for protection from ultraviolet rot. There are, however, two weights of Dacron cover cloth that are nothing more than unfinished sailcloth that is given ultraviolet protection. I have not found this material satisfactory for general canvas work since its high thread count results in a fabric that tears relatively quickly.

---

*__Acrylan__ is a registered trademark of the Monsanto Company for its line of acrylic fibers. __Dacron__ is a registered trademark of the Du-Pont Company for its line of polyester fibers. Both materials are available from other companies so the generic terms are used in the text, even though the trade names are probably better known.

Nylon

Nylon fibers are not very resistant to sun rot. Indeed, nylon exposed two years in the sun will be so brittle and faded as to be practically useless. Yet nylon is extremely strong and resistant to abrasion. It is also easily and inexpensively vat-dyed. Thus, it can be used in relatively light weights for some products at a very reasonable comparative cost. Nylon stretches a good deal and expands when wet. Thus, if a snug and neat cover is desired, nylon should not be used—it will surely sag.

Nylon is available with a variety of finishes which make it waterproof or water-resistant and breathable. In the latter finish one can specify a very firm hand suitable for utility sails. Most canvas work will be done with a much softer cloth since it is easier to handle and very strong. This soft nylon fabric is often designated "Oxford" in light weights (six-ounce and under). "Cordura" is the trade name for an eight-ounce soft nylon of coarse texture. Note that there are variations in finish even when the fabrics have a similar hand. If the term is new to you, **hand** is the body of the fabric which defines its texture and feel. Some nylon will be coated on one side, some on both, some not at all. And the finishes themselves will vary. But the hand and the weather-proofness of the fabric are really all that concern you when ordering nylon.

CLOTH WEIGHT

Cotton canvas is available in a wide range of weights from 10 to 24 ounces per square yard. The choice is necessary because the material is generally pushed to its strength limitations in any given application. Synthetic canvas is seldom stressed to tearing in normal applications and, as a result, the range of fabric weights is quite limited. Acrylic cover fabrics are available in just one 8.3-ounce weight. Destiny 2 + 2 is made up in the same weight. The "sailcloth" Dacron cover cloth is woven in 5-ounce and 6.5-ounce weights. Weblon is 10 ounces in spite of a relatively light Dacron matrix because the vinyl laminate is quite heavy. In short there is very little choice regarding cloth weight necessary if you have already decided upon synthetic cover material!

CUTTING

After the fabric has been chosen for your project, it must be cut and sewn to proper shape. Synthetic fabrics can be cut with a wood-burning tool or a soldering tool—the heat melts the fabric and seals the cut edge to keep it from raveling. Sailmakers often use a slightly modified version of these tools and call them "hotknives" (see Figure 1). The fastest cutting method is simply to use straight shears, as you must to cut natural fiber canvas. Raveling will not be a problem as long as edges are folded under which is a general practice in all canvas work, even when edges are sealed, since a more finished appearance is achieved.

Acrylic and polyester materials will not shrink or stretch enough to require that allowance be made for it. Even treated cotton fabrics will stretch about 2%. Nylon will stretch about 3% when wet. Therefore, in the case of the latter two kinds of material, allowance should be made for stretch when cutting.

SEWING

Hand Sewing

Sewing can be done by hand or with a machine. In either case it is best to use a polyester thread. For hand sewing a much larger thread (so large that it is generally called "twine") is required and

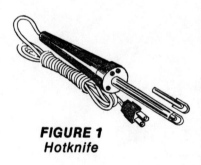

FIGURE 1
Hotknife

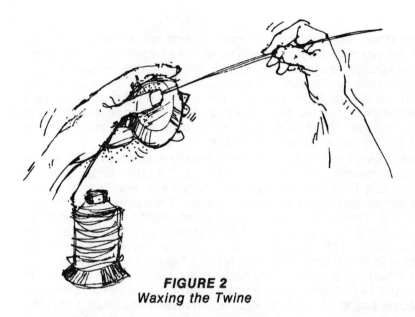

FIGURE 2
Waxing the Twine

should be waxed. Since hand sewing entails drawing the twine through the fabric again and again, waxing the twine is necessary (see Figure 2). If it were not waxed and relatively thick, it would quickly wear and chafe through. In addition to lubricating the twine, wax also strengthens it by binding the fibers together and helps prevent the stitch from coming undone if the twine breaks anywhere along its length, since it tends to lock each penetration of the cloth in place. To wax the twine simply pull it over a cake of wax several times.

Sail twine is available in several constructions, but the most versatile is a three-ply to seven-ply twisted strand. Three-ply sail twine doubled through a needle eye is generally appropriate for seaming work where two panels of fabric are to be secured together. When hardware is to be attached, the double twine can be redoubled or you can move to twine with more plys as it comes off the cone. There are no hard or fast rules about how many plys to use in any given application. Much depends upon the "look" that is preferred — the same strength can be achieved by making numerous stitches with a large twine.

Machine Sewing

When using a machine for canvas sewing, there are a few very simple rules to use in choosing proper thread and needles. For fabric of eight ounces or more, it is best to use V-92 polyester thread. For lighter weight fabric, V-69 polyester thread should be used. With the heavier thread, a #18 or #20 needle will generally work best, but a #22 is sometimes called for when working with really thick or stiff materials. With V-69 thread a #14 or #16* needle is generally best, but, once again, a larger needle should be used if any trouble is experienced.

---

*The sizes listed here are common in the United States. If you will be using a European needle, the size equivalents are: 14 = 80, 16 = 100, 18 = 110, 20 = 120, and 22 = 130.

Polyester thread tends to be somewhat more brittle and unpredictable than its cotton counterpart. Be very sure to get the best industrial thread that can be found. Heminway and Bartlett is the best that I have found—it has an excellent "sewability." If you have trouble with your thread, you can try dipping it in a silicone lubricant, or a piece of cloth soaked in the lubricant can be paper clipped over

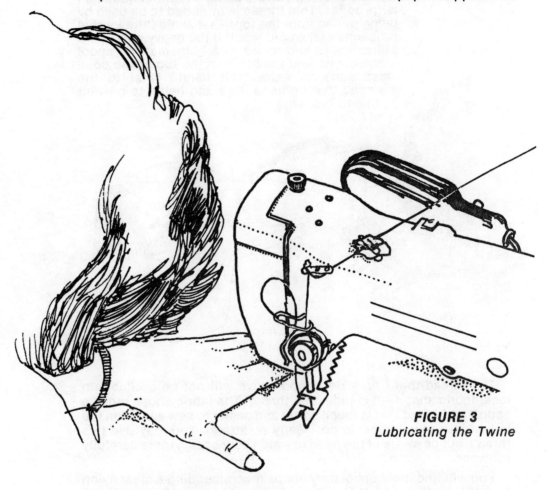

FIGURE 3
Lubricating the Twine

the top thread in the machine (see Figure 3) as it feeds to the needle.† But this should not be necessary with the Heminway and Bartlett thread.

Most canvas work is done with white thread. In part this standardization is simply convenient. But polyester is also hard to dye, and the heat necessary to make the dye fast tends to weaken the fiber and make it brittle. So, if you do decide to use colored thread, be prepared for a bit more trouble than would be normal with the white.

---

†We use an industrial sewing thread lubricant called *Clearco*. Any liquid silicone will serve the same function, but be careful to test it to make sure that it does not stain.

FIGURE 4
Using Section of Coat Hanger on
Top of Machine to Put Twist in Twine

This "clothes hanger thread guide" can be extremely useful if you are using industrial thread on large cones. That thread is intended to be used by being pulled from the top. That avoids the inertial problems that would result if the heavy cone were pulled round and round as a homemaker's spool normally is. And the lift from the top of the cone also adds an extra "left hand" twist to the thread that tightens it up and helps to prevent thread breakage.

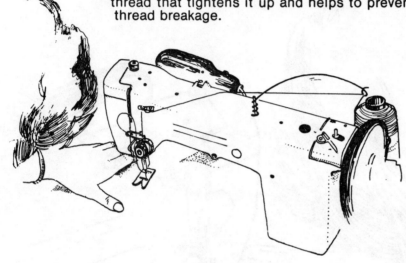

The thread that I have described above will not be available in local fabric shops—it is industrial thread. The fabric shops stock a spun fiber thread that is much softer and easier to sew with than the industrial variety, but it is not nearly so strong. You may use this thread, but be aware of the need to watch your seams more carefully for wear.

You will find most upholstery shops recommending a clear nylon monofilament thread. It is extremely easy to sew with and blends well with the color of whatever fabric you are using, but it does not hold up well in the sunlight and should thus be carefully avoided.

Stitches

There is nothing complex about the stitches used in canvas work. Whether sewing by hand or with a machine, a simple flat or "straight" stitch is appropriate. Space the stitches installed by hand on quarter inch centers. When using a machine, set it for as long a stitch as possible—at least 3/16 inch.

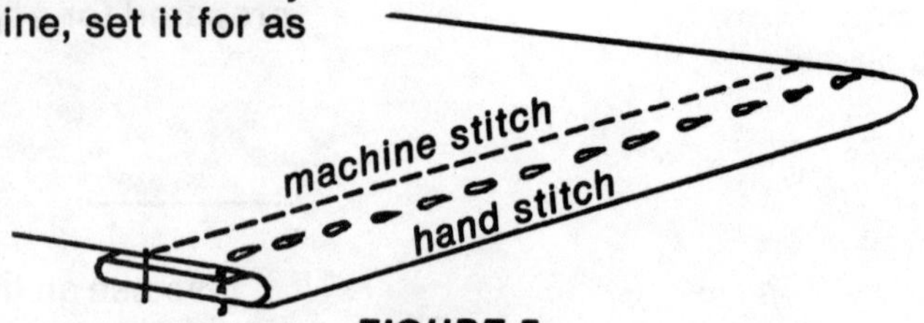

machine stitch

hand stitch

FIGURE 5
The Hand and Machine Stitches

In recommending this simple flat stitch, I am assuming that the raw edges of the fabric can be folded under to reinforce them and to keep them from raveling. The main reason for the zigzag stitch in sailmaking is that it distributes the strain well inside the unfolded fabric edge of a merely overlapped seam and also helps prevent raveling by overcasting threads along the unprotected edge. The overlapped seam, however, although necessary with very stiff Dacron sailcloth, can generally be avoided in canvas work. So long as that is the case, the straight stitch will be faster and stronger.

Note also that the acrylic materials tend to "needle pucker" when sewn along their length. This means that the mere penetration of the needle is enough to cause them to wrinkle slightly along the seam. This is generally not a serious problem—it pulls out when any stress is placed on the fabric. But the fewer times the needle penetrates the cloth, the less obvious needle pucker will be. That is one reason for using the long straight stitch in canvas work. If you want to further reduce needle pucker in acrylics, use the smallest needle possible (it must be large enough to accommodate the thread and to penetrate the material without undue breakage.)

Seams

There are any number of seams that can be used in canvas work. No one of them is "right" or better than the others. But they will offer more or less water resistance, ease of installation, and material

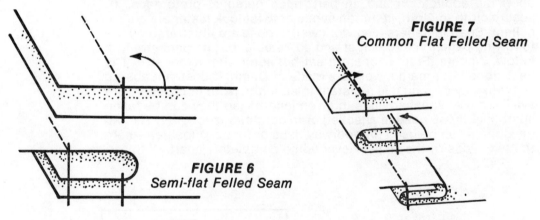

FIGURE 7
Common Flat Felled Seam

FIGURE 6
Semi-flat Felled Seam

usage. I am illustrating four possible seams for joining two cloth panels. The first is very simple. I call it a **semi-flat felled** stitch (Figure 6). It looks "finished" from one side. It is only moderately resistant to water leakage. This seam can be easily formed in two steps. First place one panel squarely on top of the other. Run a row of stitches about 1/2 inch inside the two edges to be joined. Then unfold the top panel so that only 1/2-inch seam allowance protrudes down along the seam. Fold this back against one side or the other and sew it securely with a second row of stitches.

The second is the **common flat felled** seam that is used in dressmaking (Figure 7). It is finished on both sides and highly water resistant. This stitch can be formed in one step even by beginners if the materials are first glued together with either a double-sided tape or clear silicone seal. Glue one edge directly on top of the other with an overlap of from 1/4 to 1/2 inch. Then "roll" the seam allowance over the top and unfold the panels so that the seam takes on the characteristic flat felled shape and stitch along both sides.

The third seam (Figure 8) results in a seam that looks very much like the flat felled one. It is for use with materials that do not glue well, such as Acrylan (the material is so rough in texture that the adhesives will not adhere properly). The seam is started just like the semi-flat felled one with the two panels on top of one another. The straight stitch just along their edges serves to baste them together accurately. Then the seam allowance can be rolled and the fabric unfolded to permit the final stitches.

The fourth seam (Figure 9) is started in the same way with a row of straight stitches from 1/4 to 1/2 inch inside the edges of two panels, one lying directly over the other. Then spread the panels out and press down the seam allowance so that it lies flat as shown in Figure 9. Now place a strip of polypropylene or nylon webbing over the seam allowance and secure it with a row of stitches along both edges of the webbing. Be careful to baste the webbing in place carefully.

Indeed, whenever you sew, don't hesitate to make good use of pins, staples, transfer tape or silicone glue to baste materials together before the actual sewing takes place. As you gain experience, this extra work will be less and less important.

FASTENERS

A number of fasteners can be used in canvas work depending upon the application and, in part, upon personal preference. To secure cloth to cloth, common sense or twist lock fasteners are excellent. Snap fasteners also work well. (These are illustrated on the following page.) Velcro is fast and adjustable, but its peel strength is low. Zippers (Figure 10) are great but somewhat expensive. The best zippers for marine work are made of Delrin. It does not absorb water like nylon, and it is resistant to sunlight. Note that zippers are available with finished ends in given lengths, so they can be taken apart (like those used in a jacket) or in continuous lengths. The latter zippers can be used for doorway flaps or for bag closures where the two sides of the zipper never come completely apart.

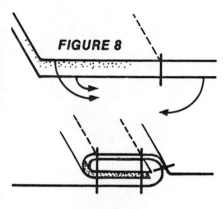

FIGURE 8

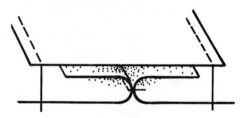

FIGURE 9
Webbing-Reinforced Seam

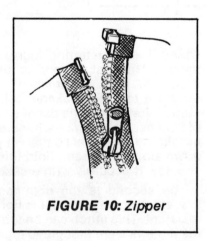

FIGURE 10: *Zipper*

To secure cloth to a surface, snap fasteners (Figure 11) are probably best, so long as stress is in shear (Figure 12). Lift-the-dot fasteners (Figure 13) are a bit more secure than snap fasteners, but a prong protrudes from the surface—it can be dangerous if tripped over or it can be ruined if bent. Common sense fasteners (Figure 14) are the most secure fasteners for cloth to surface applications, but they protrude higher than anything else. Velcro (Figure 15) can be glued to a surface as well as sewn to a fabric. It is fast and adjustable but, again, not very secure.

FINISH - NICKEL, BRASS, GOVERNMENT BLACK

BUTTON **X2-10127** 24 line 1/4 barrel length Attaching Tool 1401	**BUTTON** **X2-10128** 24 line 1/64 barrel length **XE-10105** Stainless st. cap Attaching Tool 1401	**BUTTON** **X2-10129** 20 line 3/16 barrel length Attaching Tool 1402	**SOCKET** **XB-10224** Medium action **XX-10224** Stiff action Attaching Tool 1410	**SLIDE SOCKET** **XX-10616** For use with 1/2" strap
STUD **XX-10362** No. 8-15 type "A" self-tapping screw, 3/8 and 5/8 long **XX-10393** Wood screw No. 7, 3/8 and 5/8 long Tool No. 169N hand screw driver	**STUD** **XX-10708** No. 10-32 machine screw, 1/4, 3/8, and 5/8 long Tool No. 169N hand screw driver	**STUD** **XB-10372** Use with XB-10224 for reversible combination **XX-10322** 1/4 barrel length Attaching Tool 1421	**STUD** **BS-10370** Clinch type for use with eyelet Attaching Tool 1412	**EYELET** **BS-10412** 1/4 barrel length **BS-10414** 5/16 barrel length **BS-10413** 3/8 barrel length Attaching Tool 1407

FIGURE 11: *Snap Fasteners*

FIGURE 12:
Stress in Shear and in Peel

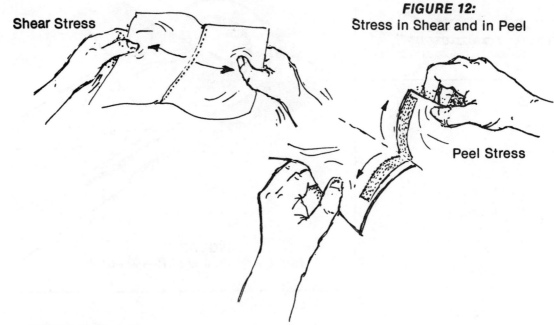

Shear Stress

Peel Stress

FIGURE 13:
Lift-the-Dot Fasteners

| SOCKET
XX-16205
Regular prong

XX-16206
Long prong

XX-16207
Socket, Military

Attaching Tool 1454
and Tool No. 9951
hand punch | CLINCH PLATE
BS-16506
For attaching
XX-16205 and
XX-16206 sockets

BS-16507
Use with XX-16207

Tool No. 1455 | STUD
BS-16349
Single, two prong
clinch type. Tool
No. 171 hand punch

CLINCH PLATE
BS-16501 | STUD
XB-16358
Single eyelet type
Attaching Tool 1456

WASHER
BS-16509

Attaching Tool 1457 | STUD
XX-16360 Single
XB-16361 Double
No. 8 wood screw
3/8 and 5/8 long

XX-16366 Single
No. 8 self-tapping
3/8 and 5/8 long

XB-16317 Single
XB-16318 Double
No.8 brass screw
3/8 and 1/2 long

XX-16362 Single
8-32 machine screw
XX-16363 Single
10-32 machine screw
1/4, 3/8 and 5/8 long

Tool No. 169B
hand screw driver |

**PRESSED TOGETHER,
THEY FASTEN TIGHTLY**

TO SEPARATE, SIMPLY PEEL APART

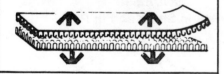

FIGURE 15:
Velcro

Purchase points for tying the fabric in place can be simple loops of webbing sewn in place in the Box-X stitch, illustrated in Figure 16. Brass or stainless steel rings inserted in the loops will

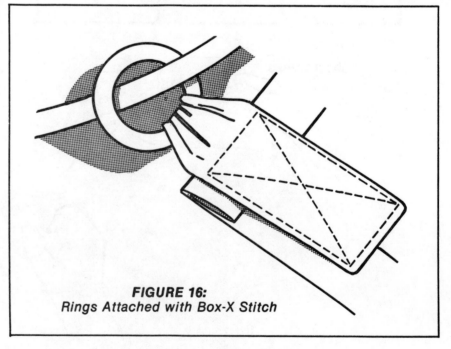

FIGURE 16:
Rings Attached with Box-X Stitch

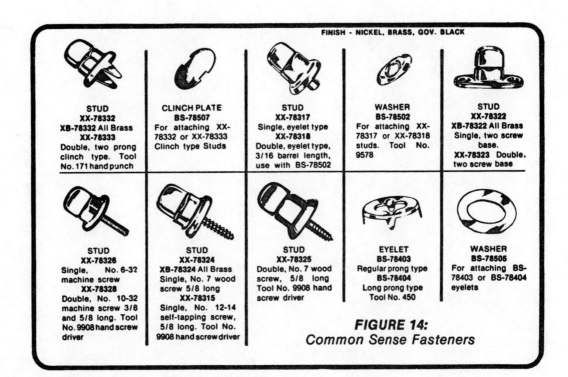

FINISH - NICKEL, BRASS, GOV. BLACK

STUD
XX-78332
XB-78332 All Brass
XX-78333
Double, two prong clinch type. Tool No. 171 hand punch

CLINCH PLATE
BS-78507
For attaching XX-78332 or XX-78333 Clinch type Studs

STUD
XX-78317
Single, eyelet type
XX-78318
Double, eyelet type, 3/16 barrel length, use with BS-78502

WASHER
BS-78502
For attaching XX-78317 or XX-78318 studs. Tool No. 9578

STUD
XX-78322
XB-78322 All Brass
Single, two screw base.
XX-78323 Double, two screw base

STUD
XX-78326
Single, No. 6-32 machine screw
XX-78328
Double, No. 10-32 machine screw 3/8 and 5/8 long. Tool No. 9908 hand screw driver

STUD
XX-78324
XB-78324 All Brass
Single, No. 7 wood screw 5/8 long
XX-78315
Single, No. 12-14 self-tapping screw, 5/8 long. Tool No. 9908 hand screw driver

STUD
XX-78325
Double, No. 7 wood screw, 5/8 long Tool No. 9908 hand screw driver

EYELET
BS-78403
Regular prong type
BS-78404
Long prong type Tool No. 450

WASHER
BS-78505
For attaching BS-78403 or BS-78404 eyelets

FIGURE 14:
Common Sense Fasteners

FIGURE 17: Grommets

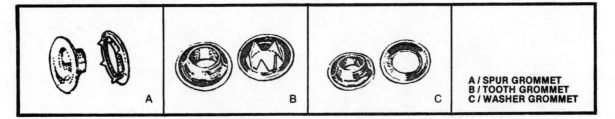

A / SPUR GROMMET
B / TOOTH GROMMET
C / WASHER GROMMET

be somewhat easier to tie to. And, of course, grommets (Figure 17) are commonly used. They are quickly installed with proper tools, and their low cost makes them the choice of professionals. Note that there are three main types of grommets for canvas work. There are the "common washer grommets." These are the light-duty grommets that you find in most hardware stores. "Tooth grommets" are made with spikes that penetrate the fabric round the outside of the grommet washers and lock it in place. "Spur grommets" have similar spikes, but they are given rolled edges that further reduce the possibility of grommets tearing out. Common washer grommets are satisfactory for most boat canvas work, but there is no doubt of the superiority of spur grommets. You must use your judgment in making grommet selection based on the stress that any given grommet is likely to confront.

This section has served to introduce the principles of canvas work. In the other sections which follow I will develop specific instructions for the construction of particular items. You need not read those in order of presentation—pick what interests you most and start there.

2

Awnings
and
Enclosures

AWNINGS AND ENCLOSURES

Awnings and enclosures, the fabric structures under consideration here, are intended to provide protection. Whether protection from hot sun or blustery cold winds, the fabric called upon to provide it must be durable and strong as well as wind and water tight.

The fabrics appropriate for awning use follow:

1. A vinyl/polyester laminated fabric is especially useful here. It is relatively inexpensive (about the price of pure polyester) and yet very durable in sunlight and perfectly waterproof. It is also easy to keep clean. Perhaps the most significant advantage of the vinyl coated fabric is its 62-inch width which reduces waste and sewing time.

2. The acrylic fabrics look better (they have more bulk and thus hide wrinkles better). And, of course, their durability is excellent. But they are not easy to fold into a small bundle and store.

3. Indeed, if storage is a primary concern and if the awning is intended just for "fair weather" use, 1.5-ounce ripstop nylon should be considered. But note that the nylon is not so strong or durable as could be desired.

4. A recent entry in the awning fabric category is "Rollafurl" from Bainbridge. This three-ounce coated Dacron is waterproof and highly resistant to ultraviolet deterioration. It is available in a wide range of bright colors on one side (the underside is always white). "Rollafurl" is 58 inches wide. For many it will be the perfect compromise between the heavy vinyl material and the flimsy nylon fabrics.

The other materials needed for awnings and enclosures will vary a good deal. Thread, of course, is universal—V-69 is the proper choice. Fasteners can range from simple webbing loops or loops of webbing with rings in place through twist-locks and lift-the-dots to Delrin zippers and Velcro. Personal preference and the circumstances confronted in meeting particular needs should guide your choice.

I am going to present detailed instructions here for a simple flat sun shade awning. Then I am going to suggest some common modifications which are often made on this basic design to either improve its simple shielding function or to provide a more complete enclosure.

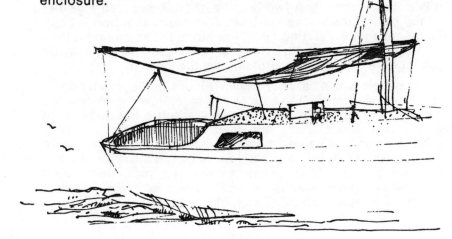

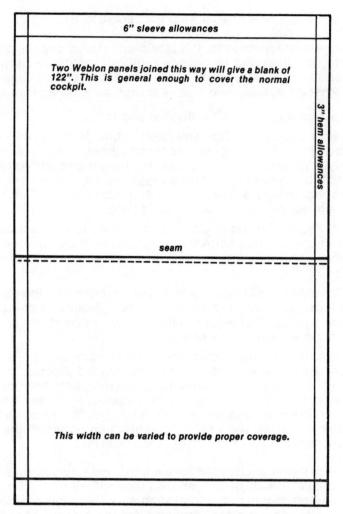

FIGURE 1
A Representative Awning Pattern

The basic pattern for a flat awning is shown in Figure 1. Notice that it is nothing more than two lengths of cloth secured together so that the seam runs across the boat. This seam direction is best, since it means that water runoff will flow along the seam rather than into it. With narrower cloths, three or even four panels can be secured together to provide approximately the same awning length.

Join the panels with a flat felled seam (Figure 2). Place two panels directly over one another, top side to top side. Sew them together with a row of the longest possible straight stitches about 1½ inch inside the two edges. Fold the seam allowance up and over twice—at the same time bring the lower panel out so that the seam is formed as shown in the figure below. Now run a row of straight stitches along the folded edges nearest to your first stitch line—this will hold the seam allowance in place for the next row of straight stitches along the other side of the seam.

This entire seaming operation will be easier if you make good use of pins or double sided tape or clear silicone adhesive to baste the material before it is sewn. The problem is that the fabric layer on the bottom tends to move through the machine faster than that on the top. After all, the feed dog teeth touch only the bottom layer. An experienced operator can overcome this problem, but a little care can yield a job comparable to that of the most skilled craftsman.

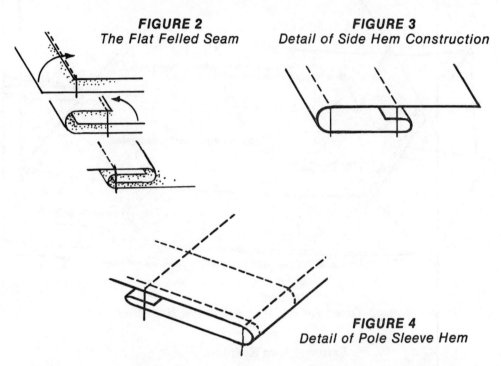

FIGURE 2
The Flat Felled Seam

FIGURE 3
Detail of Side Hem Construction

FIGURE 4
Detail of Pole Sleeve Hem

Next fashion 2½-inch hems along the sides of the cover (Figure 3). To install these hems, simply crease the fabric sharply along a hem fold line 3 inches inside the sides of the cover blank. Place a row of straight stitches within 1/4 inch of the fold to hold the hem in place. Then run another row of straight stitches along the inside edge of the hem after rolling under 1/2 inch of the fabric to finish the inside edge of the hem. Use #465 double sided adhesive tape or staples and pins to hold the material in place and keep it from sliding. I find that slippage is a much less serious problem if the flap of the hem is folded underneath the rest of the cover as it is run through the machine. This enables the machine's feed dog to engage both the hem and the bulk of the material.

The leading and trailing edges of the awning can be finished with sleeves for spreader poles or they can be finished with 2½ inch hems like the sides if poles are either not to be used or if they are to be external to the awning.

If sleeves are desired, they should be from 4 to 6 inches wide. They are, in effect, large hems open at their ends (Figure 4) so that supporting poles can be inserted (Figure 5 below—which will also show external pole systems). Make them up in the same way you did the smaller 2½-inch ones above, but place the first row of stitches within 1/8 inch of the hem crease at the very edge of the awning so that it will not interfere with the insertion of the poles. It is not a good idea to leave this first stitch out since it holds the fabric in place for the inner row of stitches and helps to prevent wrinkles.

Often a sleeve or two is desired through the center of the awning. This can be provided for by simply sewing a 4 to 6 inch wide strip of material to the underside of the awning. First fold under the ends and the two long sides to provide 1/4-inch hems all round. Then carefully pin, tape, or glue the strip to the awning underside. Sew it in place with a row of straight stitches along both edges.

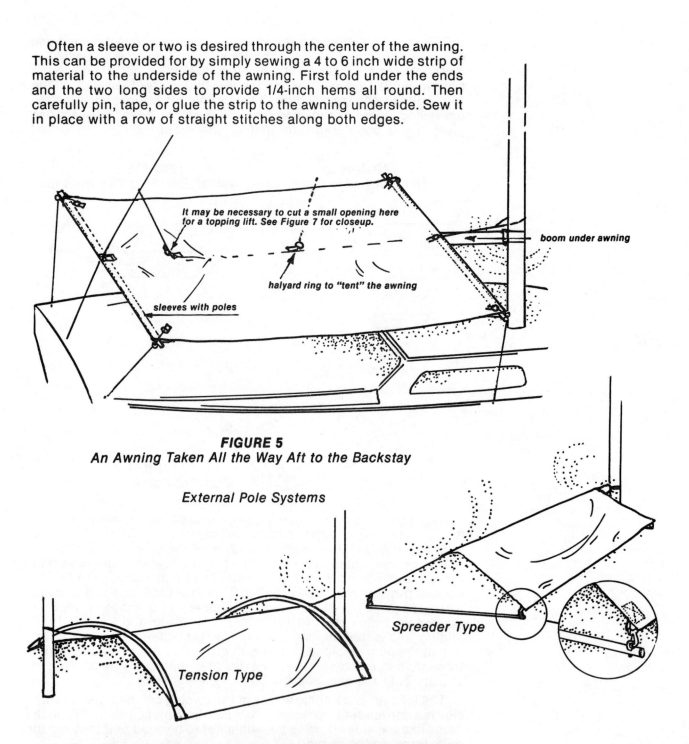

It may be necessary to cut a small opening here for a topping lift. See Figure 7 for closeup.

boom under awning

halyard ring to "tent" the awning

sleeves with poles

FIGURE 5
An Awning Taken All the Way Aft to the Backstay

External Pole Systems

Tension Type

Spreader Type

In the place of sleeves, you may want to use external spreader poles or perhaps you may be able to eliminate poles entirely. There are two systems for external pole support shown with Figure 5. One of these entails bending the poles over the top of the awning and inserting their ends into pockets formed by sewing webbing tapes to the surface of the fabric. These pockets are generally two-inch polypropylene webbing folded in half and stitched in place along both sides. First, however, fold over about 1/4 inch of the ends of the webbing strip and sew them down in order to prevent raveling.

The second external pole system makes use of poles to simply spread the material. All that is required here is a system to secure the ends of the poles to the corners of the awning, such as eyescrews in the pole ends which are snapped in place at the four corners of the awning. In other respects, the awning with poles suspended underneath will not be structurally different from one that is simply stretched over the boom from one side of the boat to another.

On bigger boats it is seldom necessary to have poles at the ends of an awning. Here the material can be finished with 2½-inch hems all around. Rings or grommets can be installed along the edges, and the material can be stretched from lifeline to lifeline over the boom.

It is possible to buy special telescoping aluminum poles. They work very well. My preference, however, is for the fiber glass rods that are usually available in camping supply stores (where they are sold for tent poles). Indeed, they even come with sleeves so that they come apart, minimizing storage problems. Aluminum conduit also works well. Sleeves are available here to permit breaking the poles down. And, of course, there are the old standbys: bamboo or ash or hickory poles.

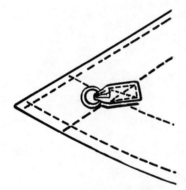

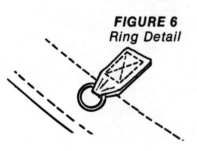

FIGURE 6
Ring Detail

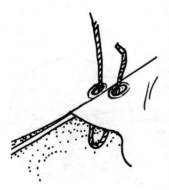

There must be some way to support the awning. That support is often provided by the boom. This is especially useful if a topping lift can be used to raise the boom high enough to give proper headroom. Sometimes it is desirable to suspend an awning from its forward and aft edges without any support from the rigid boom. If this is your plan and your awning is more than 20 feet long, consider sewing a supporting rope down the backbone of the material. Fold the fabric underside to underside in half down its length and insert a 1/4-inch Dacron rope into the fold (it should be about a foot longer than the awning on both ends so that eyes can be spliced into the ends). Sew the rope into the fold with the zipper foot attachment on your machine. This rope can then be stretched fore and aft to provide support without straining the material in the awning. Note that any sleeves crossing the support rope must be made up in two halves.

One other feature of the basic awning remains to be considered. There must be some means by which it can be secured to the boat. The simplest way to tie a line to the fabric is to sew a webbing loop in place. By placing a brass or stainless ring in this loop (Figure 6), you can make it easier to pass a line through. Grommets are fast and relatively inexpensive, but they do require a rather expensive installation tool and, besides, it is not always possible to place grommets conveniently when free passage through a sleeve must be preserved.

The placement of tie points in the awning will depend upon your particular requirements. Nevertheless, it is possible to say that "normal" locations include all four corners and the centers of the leading and trailing edges. One tie point in the center of the awning can be used to give the fabric a peak. Simply attach the halyard and lift the awning a few inches. If your awning has a support rope down its backbone, any center ties should use grommets so the tie can be made around the rope—a bridle can be fashioned. The accompanying figure illustrates the "normal" tie point locations and this bridle rig.

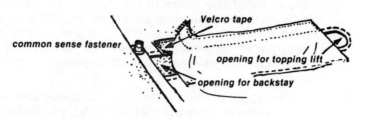

FIGURE 7
Detail of a Split Awning

Velcro tape

common sense fastener

opening for topping lift

opening for backstay

MODIFICATIONS

This simple awning can be modified any number of ways. If the boom is too short to support the awning all the way aft over the cockpit, you may want to slit the aft edge of the awning in order to pass it around the topping lift that supports the boom (Figure 7). Cut this slit before forming the aft pole sleeve or hem. Line it with a length of binding tape or leather. Then fashion the sleeve or hem as directed above. This opening will enable the awning to be pulled around the topping lift and onto the backstay.

A flap may be sewn to one side of the slit and a Velcro closure used to secure its other side if leaks are likely to be a problem. In some cases, it will be necessary to use a twist lock fastener and a tab to securely link the ends of the slit together again (this will be so when external poles are used, since there will be considerable tension across the awning). Figure 7 illustrates this application.

Perhaps the most common modification to an awning is the addition of skirts which can be rolled up tightly under the awning eaves or dropped down and tied to the deck to provide more complete protection. These skirts should be made up of a single panel along each side where the protection is desired. Hem them on all four sides and secure them to the finished edges of the flat awning with a couple rows of straight stitches as shown in the the next illustration with closeups, Figure 8. Slip 12-inch lengths of 3/4- or one-inch webbing into the seams on roughly three-foot centers as shown below. These can be used to secure the rolled-up skirt in place.

FIGURE 8
Side Panel Attachment Detail

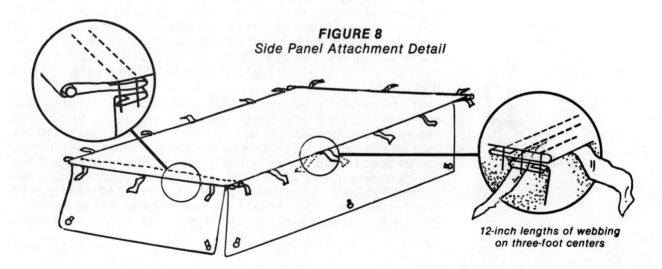

12-inch lengths of webbing
on three-foot centers

If even more protection is desired, twist-lock fasteners or zippers can be installed to close the ends of the skirts at each corner. Webbing loops, snap fasteners, rings, or grommets can be used to secure the lower edge of each skirt along the deck.

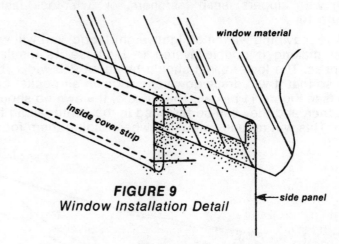

FIGURE 9
Window Installation Detail

Plasti-Pane window material (.019-inch is the normal thickness for this application) or mosquito netting can be sewn in place, if desired (Figure 9). Whichever material is used, secure it carefully to the inside surface with #465 transfer tape and/or pins before sewing. Then sew it with a single row of zigzag stitches all around its edge. Only then should the cover fabric be cut. Leave one inch of extra material to fold under and, thus, finish the outside lip of the window. Sew this lip down with another zigzag stitch. A narrow (two-inch or so) tape of the same fabric as the rest of the awning with finished edges can be sewn all around the edge of the plastic or netting on the inside to give it a finished appearance.

FIGURE 10
A Tent Awning with a Three-Gore Aft End

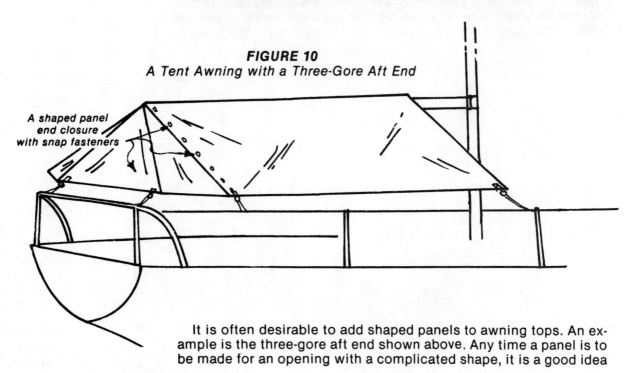

It is often desirable to add shaped panels to awning tops. An example is the three-gore aft end shown above. Any time a panel is to be made for an opening with a complicated shape, it is a good idea to make a pattern first, using newspaper or wrapping paper. Tape the paper in place and trim it until you achieve a perfect fit. Don't forget to provide a hem allowance when you cut the cover fabric. Seam the shaped structure just like the rest of the awning and attach with zippers, snap fasteners, or twist-lock fasteners (see Figure 10).

If your awning will be of lightweight fabric, you will want to consider making it double-layered to increase its insulating effectiveness. The lower panel should be about 2% wider than the top one so that it will drape down and form an air pocket between the two (see Figure 11 below). The sides of the awning should be sewn together, and they can be fastened in the center along their length also. This will reduce confusion when folding them for storage.

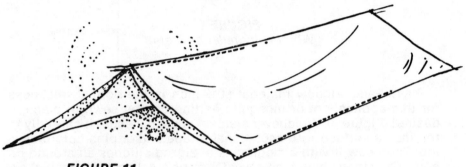

FIGURE 11
Double-Layered Tent Awning

Don't hesitate to depart radically from the basic designs that I have presented here. Each awning or enclosure will present its own unique problems. Use imagination and common sense in dealing with them.

3

Boat Covers

BOAT COVERS

Boat covers, like sail covers, should be made of a fabric that breathes so that condensation will not form on the underside. And they should be resistant to sunlight, stretch, and abrasion. The polyester and acrylic fabrics best meet these requirements.

Vinyl laminated polyester fabric can be used. It is, after all, perfectly waterproof. And proper ventilation can prevent mildew problems. I will describe some effective ventilation techniques below.

In addition to fabric, you need thread, fasteners, leather, and line. The thread should be #69 polyester—usually white for strength and sewability. A number of fasteners can be used depending upon your application.

Indeed, it is important to determine which fastening system will be used before beginning work on the cover since that will determine how much the fabric will overlap the gunwales.

★ For small dinghys with bumpers all round, it is generally sufficient to fabricate a casing in the cover edge with a drawstring that can be used to gather the cover in under the edge of the bumper.

★ An alternative is cloth to surface snap fasteners secured at 18 to 28 inch intervals all round the boat. Lift-the-dot fasteners work well here also except that I find them more likely to break off the boat since they protrude a bit farther.

★ Larger boats, especially those that will be trailered with the cover in place, can make good use of a more secure system—line can be run from side to side under the boat.

★ Boats left in the water that have numerous obstacles to a drawstring like stays and shrouds, can make use of weighted bags to hold the cover in place.

Also plan now for any ridge pole installation. Ridge poles increase the effectiveness of the cover by reducing the tendency for rain water to pool. They also increase air circulation under the cover, reducing the likelihood of condensation.

There are three types of ridge poles: 1) those extending from side to side across the boat, 2) those running fore and aft, and 3) those used vertically like a tent pole to form a peak in the cover. Depending upon the ridgepole used (or even whether one is used) more or less fabric will be required.

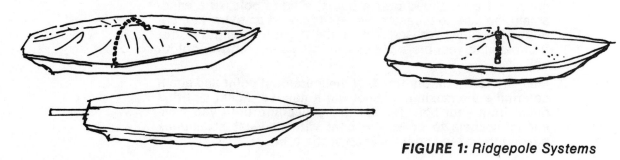

FIGURE 1: *Ridgepole Systems*

It is not possible for me to recommend one fastening system or one type of ridge pole. The choice must always be made in light of a consideration of the requirements of the cover in question. Read over this section and the "Principles of Canvas Work" section before making your decision.

Boat covers must of necessity be custom fitted. In spite of this, they are all constructed in essentially the same way, and the construction steps are remarkably easy. The five steps to a finished boat cover are carefully described below. Read these instructions carefully before proceeding. The peculiarities of the cover you have in mind may require an alternative method or technique here and there. Nevertheless, these instructions will provide the principles of construction which you will need.

I. First construct the basic cloth "blank." The blank is a rough piece of fabric that will cover the boat with an extra allowance for fitting and finishing. It is usually made up of thwartship panels since rain can be more easily shed when it runs along seams rather than into them. (I assume a cover with its highest point along the center line.) But, especially with small boats, you may want to cut panels that run fore and aft in order to simplify construction and minimize waste. In either case, principles of construction will be similar.

    A. Measure the boat by running a line from the bow to stern down its center.

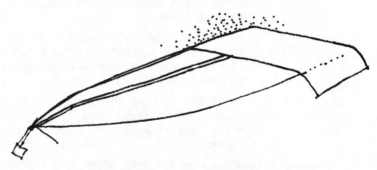

FIGURE 2: *Measurement Procedure*

    B. Allow roughly six inches of extra cloth below the lowest cover position on the side of the boat all around. Measure forward from the transom the width of the cloth panel you are using (after seaming), less the extra six inches' allowance and any overhang. Determine the width of the boat at this point. If your cover will be dropped over a boom, a ridge pole, or a windshield, be sure to measure over its top. Add an extra 12-inch allowance plus overhang. This is the maximum length of the first panel in your cloth blank. Cut this panel from your cloth bolt.

    C. Measure forward from this first measurement point and again determine the maximum panel width needed. Again, cut this panel from your bolt. Repeat this procedure until you have enough panels to cover the boat with at least six inches beyond the overhang allowance at the bow.

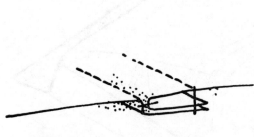

FIGURE 3: *Seaming Detail*

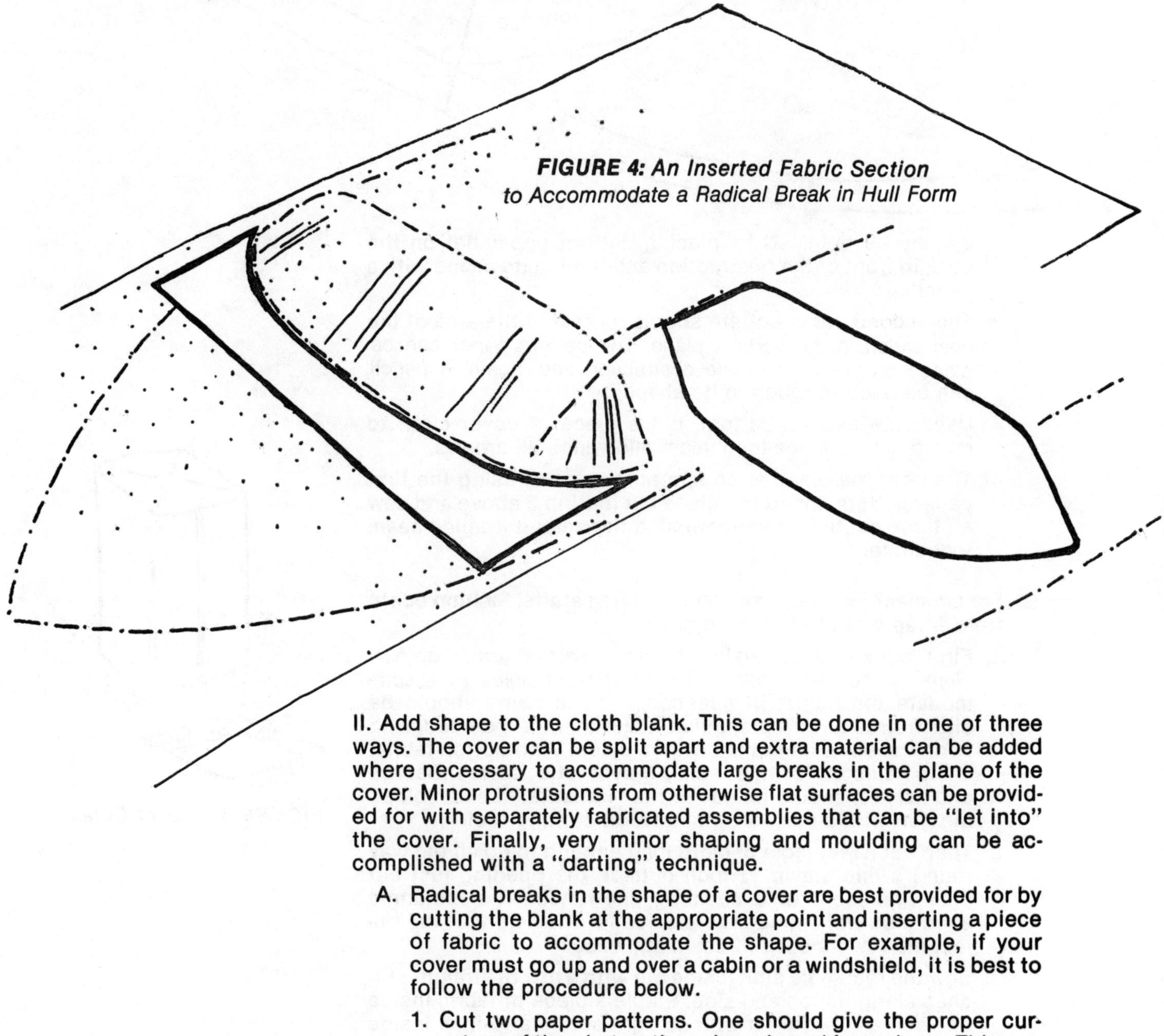

D. Sew your panel sections together in their order of measurement. Use a blind stitch (also called semi-flat felled): place the two panels to be joined one directly over the other. Take care that each panel is centered over its neighbor. Place a row of straight stitches ½-inch inside the edges of the panels where they are to be joined. Now open the sewn panels out and spread them flat. Fold over the "seam allowance" (a double layer ½-inch of cloth protruding beyond the joined pieces) and sew it to the cover with a line of stitches (straight stitches are perfectly satisfactory). The finished seam will have a cross section like that represented in Figure 3.

FIGURE 4: *An Inserted Fabric Section to Accommodate a Radical Break in Hull Form*

II. Add shape to the cloth blank. This can be done in one of three ways. The cover can be split apart and extra material can be added where necessary to accommodate large breaks in the plane of the cover. Minor protrusions from otherwise flat surfaces can be provided for with separately fabricated assemblies that can be "let into" the cover. Finally, very minor shaping and moulding can be accomplished with a "darting" technique.

A. Radical breaks in the shape of a cover are best provided for by cutting the blank at the appropriate point and inserting a piece of fabric to accommodate the shape. For example, if your cover must go up and over a cabin or a windshield, it is best to follow the procedure below.

1. Cut two paper patterns. One should give the proper curvature of the obstruction when viewed from above. This can

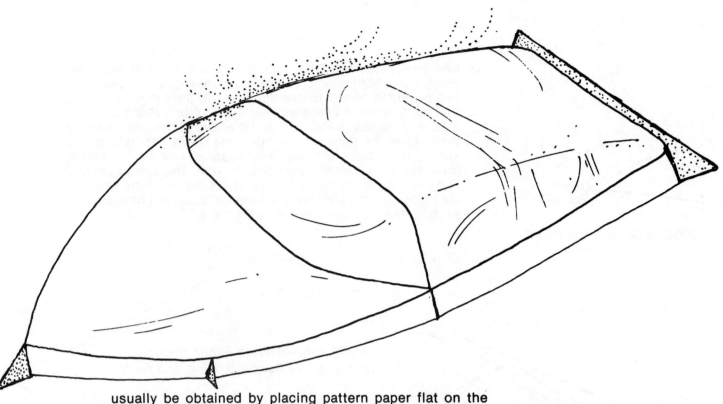

usually be obtained by placing pattern paper flat on the deck in front of the obstruction and tracing its shape with a pencil.

2. The second paper pattern should represent the area of the obstruction in the vertical plane. The pattern paper can be placed on the front of the obstruction and, again, a pencil can be used to rough in its shape.

3. Using the second pattern, cut a piece of cover cloth to match. Allow a one-inch seam allowance all around.

4. Then cut the blank at an appropriate point using the first paper pattern. Insert the piece cut in Step 3 above and sew all three sections together using the semi-flat felled seam technique.

B. For smaller obstacles like lights and flag staffs, fashion boots from scrap cloth to fit the object.

1. First mark the underside of the cover at each object. Remove the blank from the boat and cut holes to accommodate the object in question. These holes should be either circular or rectangular. Make them large enough to permit easily sliding the cover in place. With cotton fabric, use a scissors for this task. All synthetic fabrics (Dacron and acrylic) should be cut with a "hotknife," i.e., a soldering gun with a narrow tip or a wood burning tool.

FIGURE 5: *Pocket Detail*

2. Then cut a rectangle of cloth long enough to go all the way round a line drawn ½ inch outside the opening just cut plus one inch for a seaming allowance. The rectangle should be wide enough to provide for the height of the object plus two inches of seam allowance.

3. Sew the rectangle shut inside out with a row of straight stitches along its top and side. Staple a piece of fabric inside one end and secure it with straight stitches ½-inch inside the barrel lip. Turn the boot right side out and insert it in the

hole cut out for it. Cut ½-inch slits in the corners of the cover hole and secure the boot to the resulting shelves of the cloth which are folded down and in (see Figure 5).

C. Minor adjustment to conform the cover to the shape of the hull can be made with "darts."

1. Indicate on the cloth with chalk, pen or pencil the size and position of darts which will cause the blank to drape properly. Simply take the fullness out of the cloth with the darts—mark the cloth with an arrow which runs down the center of the wedge of cloth which is to be removed from the cover. Also mark the maximum width of the dart at the outer edges of the cloth blank. (Some prefer to pin the cloth at the same time that it is marked.) Place all of these marks on the underside of the blank.

2. The darts need not be cut unless they are quite deep. Usually it is possible to simply fold the cloth back along the dart line. Place a row of straight stitches from the inner end of that line to the maximum width marks at the outer edge of the blank. Fold over the excess cloth in the dart and secure it with another row of stitches. The edges of the folded cloth will not be parallel unless the wedge is at right angles to them. Thus, there will be unevenness in the edges of the cloth blank after darts are sewn in. This unevenness will be taken out later.

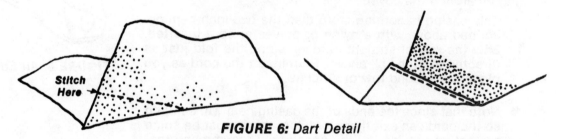

FIGURE 6: Dart Detail

3. Place the blank over the boat once more and make folds for darts on the corners of the transom. If the cover will be dropped over a high boom, there will be large darts extending to the hull at the mast. For example, if you employ a slit from the forestay to the mast, that slit will be in the shape of a large dart. This latter slit will not be sewn shut, but rather overlapped and secured with twist lock fasteners. Even so, you can trim the cloth of all excess since a tape will be applied to provide the overlap and to finish the edge.

E. Mark the cover all around the boat below the rub rail. This mark should provide the hull overlap that you have decided upon. But do add another two inches of extra cloth for one of the edge treatments described below.

III. Now the cover can be hemmed and finished.

A. There are three ways to finish the edges of a cover. First, it can simply be hemmed. Any fasteners or weights can be installed along this reinforced edge. Second, it can be finished to provide a casing for a drawstring. And, third, it can be finished with a tabling if there is a good deal of curve in the edge. The tabling can be for purposes of hardware installation or for a drawstring casing. You should go to Step 1, 2, or 3 below depending upon the edge desired.

1. To provide a **simple hem**, fold over the two inches of extra cloth provided for in Step E above. Hems are appropriate whenever covers will be fastened or hung in place rather than tied with a drawstring. Hems provide a reinforced edge around the cover into which fasteners can be secured.

    a. Cut the cloth all around on your mark. Use your hotknife unless the cover is cotton. If scissors are used, make the hem a double fold by installing a ½-inch hem prior to the main one.

    b. Crease the cover well along its edge by folding it over and pressing it down firmly with a heavy, flat object like an old iron—do not use heat on synthetic materials.

    c. Sew the hem in the cover edge by running a row of straight stitches along the outer fold. A second row should then be placed along the inside edge of the hem.

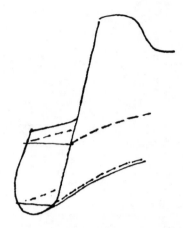

FIGURE 7: A Simple Hem

2. If your cover has no slits for shrouds or stays, it will be possible to secure it with a drawstring that is fitted in a **casing** all around the cover.

    a. This casing is nothing more than the two-inch hem described above with a nylon or polyester cord inserted. Sew the row of straight stitches along the fold just as directed in Step "c" above. Then insert the cord as you place the second row of stitches.

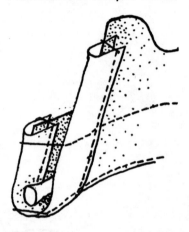

FIGURE 8: An Edge Casing

    b. Note that since the ends of the casing hem will be open so the cord can exit them for tying, there must be some protection provided at the openings. I recommend that you use vinyl binding tape or strips of leather to accomplish this. Sew these protective strips in place before finishing the stitching along the casing. Or you may prefer to install grommets near the ends of the casing and use these for the cord to exit. Then the casing can be closed along all edges just like the hem above.

3. Finally, it is possible to use a **tabling** to accomplish either of the two finishing techniques described above. A tabling should be used whenever the edge of the cover has one or more relatively radical curves. Hems will always require that the cloth be wrinkled when sharp curves are encountered. Tabling eliminates these wrinkles by using a covering tape that is cut in the same shape as the cover edge itself. It is made possible by cutting away the two-inch hem allowance and lifting it up and over on top of the new cover edge. Fold under both edges of the tabling tape first and sew them in place. Then fold over the edge of the cover itself and sew it in place. All of these protective hems can be very narrow—¼-inch is fine. Sew the tabling in

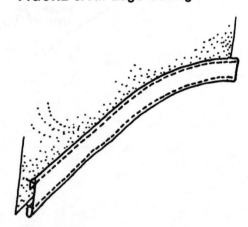

FIGURE 9: An Edge Tabling

place with two rows of straight stitches—one along each edge. Don't forget to insert the cord if you will be using a drawstring.

B. If the cover will have slits to provide for the mast or for shrouds, you will want to make it possible to overlap and seal the cloth along those slits. This can be done by securing a tape along both edges of the slits.

1. This tape should be cut from scrap cloth. Make it 1½ inches longer than the slit. Cut it six inches wide and fold it in half lengthwise to make a three-inch wide strip. Sew the folded tape with a row of straight stitches down its center, starting and ending the row about ¾ inch from the ends of the tape (see stitch # 1 in Figure 10). Place the folded strip over the raw slit edges. There will be a total overlap of 1½ inches along the slit. Then secure the tape to these edges with two rows of stitches (either zigzag or straight will do).

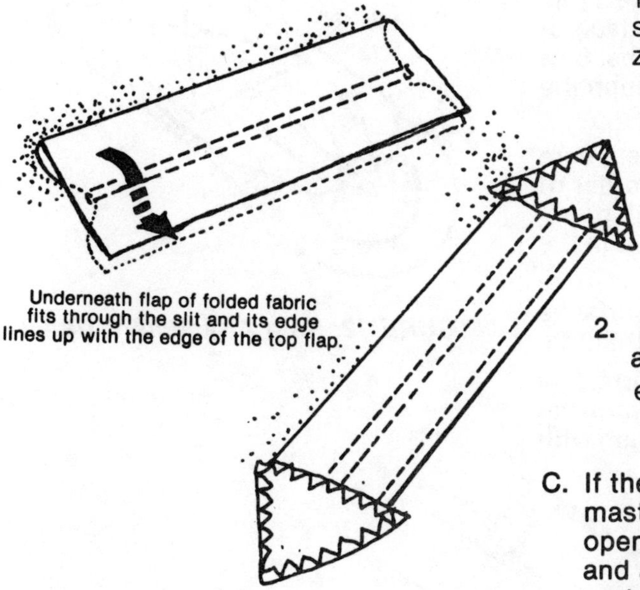

Underneath flap of folded fabric fits through the slit and its edge lines up with the edge of the top flap.

FIGURE 10: *Procedure for Finishing Slit Edges with Tape*

2. At the apex of the slits and along curved edges (such as around shroud plates) use pearl grey leather to protect the edges from wear (see Figure 10).

C. If there are any protrusions that will not be covered such as a mast, a "wrap around boot" should be made up to seal that opening. Such boots are generally from six to ten inches high and are long enough to wrap from 1½ to 2 times around the protrusion.

1. Place ¼-inch hems in all four sides of the boot rectangle.
2. Then sew the boot to the opening in the cover. Lay the outside surface of the boot against the outside surface of the cover and run a row of straight stitches ¼-inch inside the two edges. Keep the edges flush as you move all round the cover opening. This will require careful positioning since the straight side of the boot must be made to go round the very "unstraight" opening, but it can be done and it will look good when you are done.

IV. Now place fastenings in the cover so that it can be pulled tight and kept that way. All cloth to cloth fastening will require the overlap tapes described in Section III/B above.

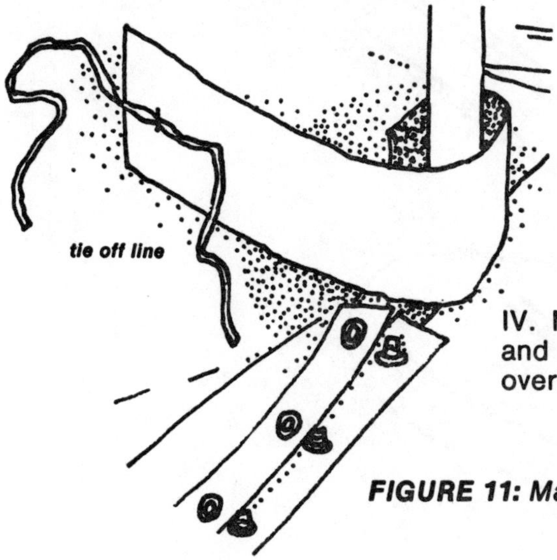

tie off line

FIGURE 11: *Mast Boot Detail*

A. Twist-lock or "common-sense" fasteners are installed with a small pen knife. Press the fastener stud or socket onto the cloth where it is to be placed so that its prongs leave slight indentations. Make a small slit in the cloth with the point of your knife over these indentations. It is a good idea to heat the knife blade before making the slit (if the fabric is synthetic) so that it will be well sealed. Insert the prongs of the stud or socket through these slits and place an appropriate backing plate inside. Then bend the prongs over onto the backing plate with a pair of pliers.

B. Lift-the-dot fasteners are installed in the same fashion as common sense fasteners.

C. The common sense or lift-the-dot fasteners will keep the cover secure while the boat is at the dock, but if the cover is to be used while trailering, it is a good idea to tie ropes from one side on the cover to the other around the hull of the boat. Several rings should be sewn to the outside hem surface of the cover with a loop of cloth folded to three thicknesses. Sew the loop of cloth to the cover with several passes through the machine so that it is quite secure.

D. Grommets can also be used to provide tie down points. There are three types of grommets available. In ascending order of quality they are: (1) common washer grommets, (2) teeth grommets, and (3) rolled rim spur grommets. I prefer the latter in the #2 size for boat covers.

E. Velcro can be sewn to fabric pieces and glued to surfaces wherever needed. Sew around all edges with a straight stitch.

F. If you desire to install a zipper, first break it in two parts. Lay each part on top of the cover with the teeth *away from* the opening to be closed and the cloth zipper tape edge flush with

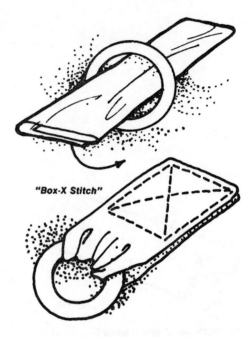

"Box-X Stitch"

FIGURE 12: *Ring Attachment Detail*

FIGURE 13: *Detail of Zipper Installation*

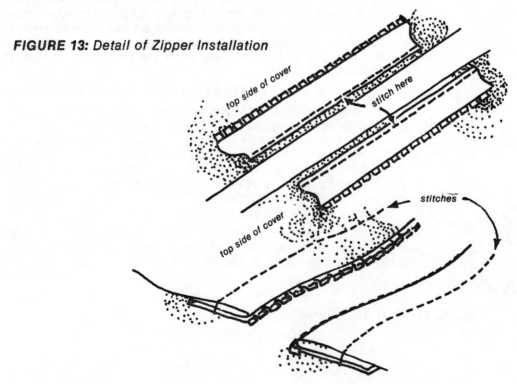

top side of cover

stitch here

top side of cover

stitches

the fabric opening edge. Sew both zipper tapes to the zipper teeth. Then fold the zippers under so that the teeth face each other. Fold the material back far enough so that there is a flap of cloth provided to partially cover the zipper. Sew the fold in place with straight stitches. Note that zipper installation makes full use of the 1½-inch overlap provided in Step III/B.

G. For some covers used over boats left in the water, where it is desirable to avoid any fastenings in the toe rails or along the side of the boat, you will want to fashion sand bags along the edges of the cover and let their weight hold it in place. These bags should be roughly 12 inches by five inches finished. Make them from strips of fabric 25 inches by six inches. Fold the strips down their center (across their narrow dimension). Insert two strips of webbing or hemmed fabric as shown in Figure 8. Then sew the two long edges with a straight stitch just a half-inch inside the fabric edges. Turn the bag inside out, fill it with clean sand and sew the open end shut with a straight stitch after folding the raw edges inside. The two exposed strips should be used to secure the bags to the edge of the cover at roughly 30-inch intervals.

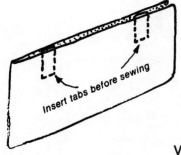

FIGURE 14: *Tab Placement in Weight Bags*

V. Place leather patches on the underside of the cover wherever it rests against a part of the boat. This will protect it from wear. Not all machines will sew leather well. If you have trouble, do the work by hand. Use a sailmaker's needle and waxed five-ply twine to accomplish this.

Test your cover for final fit. Take the time to make minor adjustments—they will greatly prolong the life of the cover and improve its appearance at the same time. If there are any places where the cover is not well secured, add fasteners or tie lines as necessary.

4

Bosun's Chairs

THE BOSUN'S CHAIR

Bosun's chairs can generally be placed in one of two categories: hard bottom and soft bottom. The former are often no more than boards with a sling attached or they can be very fancy indeed with tool pockets and cloth backs. In all cases, however, they suffer from a serious problem: in a rough sea, they do not feel secure. If, like me, you suffer from vertigo anyway, that little problem will be enough to keep you out of them! The soft bottom chairs hold their occupant with a vise-like grip. That reduces one's fear, but it certainly increases the discomfort of a trip aloft.

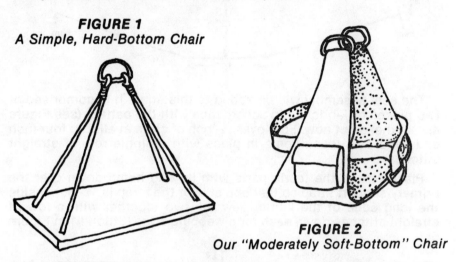

FIGURE 1
A Simple, Hard-Bottom Chair

FIGURE 2
Our "Moderately Soft-Bottom" Chair

The chair that I will describe here is a "moderately soft bottom" chair (see Figure 2). That is, it is an attempt to achieve a comfortable chair that is still safe. In essence, it is a soft bottom chair with a firm padding.

The fabric used for bosun's chairs is generally eight-ounce nylon Cordura or acrylic or Dacron cover cloth. Any of these will work quite well and serve much longer than the old chairs that were made of cotton fabrics. In addition, you will need lengths of three-inch and 1- or 1½-inch nylon or polypropylene webbing, V-69 thread, #3 D-rings, Velcro binding tape, and a piece of ½-inch thick closed cell foam padding like Ensolite.

Bosun's chairs do not have to be carefully fit, but you must be sure to make them big enough. The dimensions provided below will create a chair large enough for anyone under 230 pounds. If you need to hoist someone bigger than that, make up a test chair to determine proper dimensions.

FIGURE 3
The Primary Support Strap

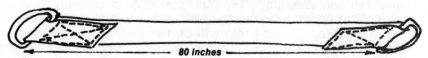

- 80 inches -

Start with a length of three-inch webbing 80 inches long (see Figure 3). Cut it with a hotknife (which can be improvised easily by using a soldering iron or gun or even a wood burning tool) to seal the ends and to keep it from raveling. Fold over three inches at each end. Place the straight side of a #3 stainless D-ring in each fold and then sew the loops of webbing with a box of straight stitches and two diagonal straight stitches (the "Box-X" stitch—see Figure 3). This webbing will be the primary support strap.

FIGURE 4
The Seat Panel Pattern

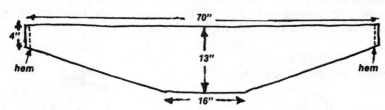

The seat assembly will be added to this strap. It is comprised of two pieces of fabric cut in accordance with the pattern (see Figure 4). Cut these out now. Fold over ½-inch of cloth at all four four-inch ends and sew these hems in place with a single row of straight stitches.

Place one of the fabric parts with its end hems down over the primary support strap so that one side of the strap is ½-inch inside the long edge of the fabric. Sew the two together with a row of straight stitches down each long webbing edge (Stitch #1 in Figure 5).

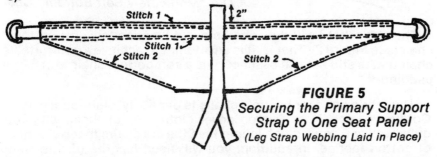

FIGURE 5
Securing the Primary Support
Strap to One Seat Panel
(Leg Strap Webbing Laid in Place)

Then hem the two sloping sides of the fabric seat panel attached to the webbing. Fold ½-inch of the material over onto the webbing side and sew it in place with a single straight stitch (Stitch #2 in Figure 5).

Place two 22-inch lengths of three-inch webbing at the center of this first seat panel and the attached webbing. These two lengths of webbing will form leg straps—they should be placed 90° to the webbing support strap. Two inches of each should protrude forward beyond the webbing (see Figure 5).

Now lay the other fabric seat panel directly on top of the panel/webbing assembly. Turn this "stack" over carefully . The webbing should be on top with the seat panel to which it is attached next in the stack. Then there will be the webbing leg straps and, finally, the second seat panel on the bottom. Place a row of straight stitches ½-inch inside the long edge of the two seat panels (Figure 6). This will, of course, mean that the stitches will be right next to the webbing. A neater job will result if you use a zipper foot on your machine—which will enable sewing right next to the webbing edge.

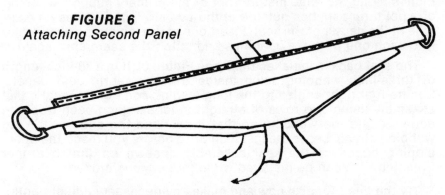

FIGURE 6
Attaching Second Panel

Note that the leg strap webbing will be sewn in place with this strip. Separate the two layers of fabric and fold the two-inch lengths of the leg webbing down onto the primary strap. Sew them in place there with a "Box-X" stitch (see Figure 7).

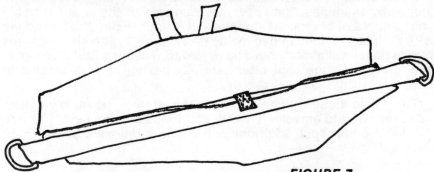

FIGURE 7
Second Panel and Leg Straps
Folded Out of the Way to Secure
Ends of Leg Straps

Then fold the bottom fabric piece all the way up and over the primary support webbing, sandwiching it neatly inside the two fabric pieces. Run two straight stitches from the corners of the 16-inch long sides of the panels to the longest edge as shown in Figure 8. Those stitches, as you will note, are perpendicular to that long edge.

FIGURE 8
The Seat Back Installation

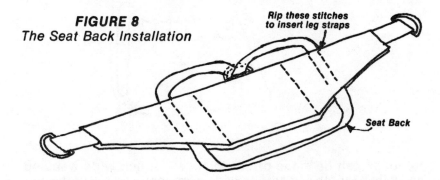

Rip these stitches
to insert leg straps

Seat Back

Now secure the leg straps to the sides of the seat assembly. First slide a #3 D-ring onto them and down to the root of the leg straps at the center of the seat. This can be used as a downhaul tie point to keep the chair steady in a breeze or at sea. Rip the stitches for three inches along the edge just in front of the primary support webbing at a point nine inches outside of the two straight stitches on each side of the center of the seat. Insert one of the leg straps two inches into each one of these openings and stitch the seam shut again.

The seat back is installed next (see Figure 8). It is a 38-inch length of three-inch webbing sewn inside the two fabric seat panels. Secure it at right angles to the long leading edge of the seat panel assembly using two rows of straight stitches along each webbing edge. Locate the webbing so that it overlaps the ends of the leg webbing straps. Leave the last inch or so before you reach the open, sloping edges of the seat assembly unsewn so that a proper finishing hem can be installed when that edge is closed.

Try the chair for size now and make any necessary adjustments.

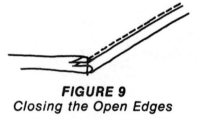

FIGURE 9
Closing the Open Edges

Slide a piece of ½-inch thick closed-cell foam, like Ensolite, into the seat bottom pocket. The foam should be a rectangle roughly 11 inches by 14 inches. Then sew the open side of the seat assembly shut with a row of straight stitches just ⅛-inch inside the two edges with their last ½-inch folded inside (see Figure 9). The sloping sides of one panel will already have been folded. You may find it easier to sew this final edge shut after carefully basting it with staples or pins.

The basic bosun's chair is finished at this point. You may, however, want to embellish it with tool loops and pockets. The normal location for such additions is just under the back strap.

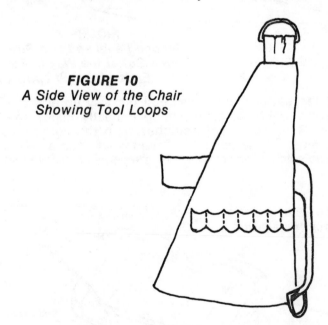

FIGURE 10
*A Side View of the Chair
Showing Tool Loops*

Tool loops can be made of one-inch or 1½-inch wide webbing. Cut an 18-inch length and sew its ends to opposite edges of the seat sides with several overlaid straight stitches. Then fasten the webbing at from four to eight points along its length, allowing it to hump up between stitches to form loops of a size appropriate for the tool you will be using (see Figure 10).

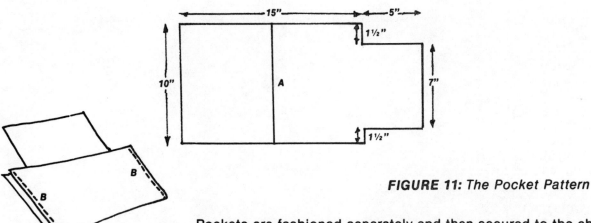

FIGURE 11: *The Pocket Pattern*

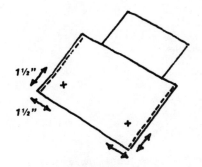

FIGURE 12
The First Step in Pocket Assembly

FIGURE 13
*Measuring for
the Pocket Bottom*

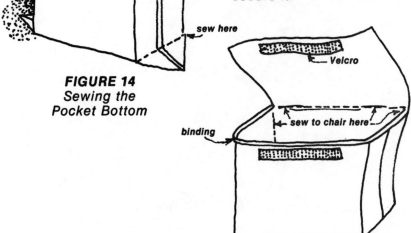

FIGURE 14
*Sewing the
Pocket Bottom*

FIGURE 15
Finishing the Pocket

Pockets are fashioned separately and then secured to the chair. For each pocket that you need, cut out a piece of fabric using as a guide the dimensions in Figure 11:

Fold the material along line "A" and sew ½-inch inside each open edge "B" with straight stitches (see Figure 12).

Measure 1½-inches up from the folded edge and in from each stitch 1½-inches. Make a small "X" on the fabric where these two measurements intersect on both sides of the pocket in each corner (see Figure 13). Pull the sides of the pocket apart at the "X" marks opposite one another and run a row of straight stitches from "X" to "X" across the corner of the pocket (see Figure 14). Do this at both corners.

Now turn the pocket inside out so that all hem allowances are hidden. Use a length of binding tape to protect the edges of the mouth of the pocket. Simply fold the binding in half along its length and use it to sandwich the raw edges. Sew the tape in place carefully with a zigzag stitch, if possible.

A short strip of Velcro tape can be separated and sewn to the pocket and to the flap of cover cloth to provide a closure (Figure 15).

Finally, sew the pocket to the bosun's chair with several overlaid straight stitches, each roughly one inch long, running four or five inches down either side of the pocket under the edges of the flap. A row of straight stitches at the hinge line of the pocket will also help to secure it.

5

Cushions and Cushion Covers

CUSHIONS AND CUSHION COVERS

Many different materials are used for boat interiors. Some are susceptible to rot and mildew. Some are not color-fast in sunlight. Needless to say, the service life of such materials is quite limited even though they can be used. I recommend a good marine cover cloth, like our Destiny II spun Dacron or our Yachtcryllic or Sunbrella Acrylans. Vinyl-coated materials, like Weblon, are fine so long as the cushion is kept dry. Because these materials do not breathe, the cushion will not dry once it becomes wet. Some prefer to use a breathing fabric on the upper surface of their cushions and the waterproof vinyl laminates on the bottom. I have experienced some mildew on the lower surface with this system, however.

The other materials needed for cushion covers are thread, binding, piping cord, and closures. V-92 or even V-69 polyester thread will give proper strength and service. Vinyl or polyester binding can be used to cover a nylon or polyester braided cord (1/8-inch or so in diameter) to form piping. Snap fasteners, common sense fasteners, Velcro, or zippers may be used for closures. If zippers are desired, the #5 or #10 Delrin zippers from YKK will give the best service—they do not corrode or rot quickly like some others.

When it comes to the materials for the cushions themselves, there is only one choice if the best is desired: a closed-cell foam like Ensolite M* or Airex**. Kapok (and other traditional marine stuffing) is satisfactory. Open-cell foams like those sold for bedding are usable and, as a matter of fact, they are the most commonly used. But these materials are the least acceptable since they tend to accumulate moisture.

If you obtain a foam for the cushion (either open- or closed-cell), the best means of cutting it is with an electric kitchen knife. If such a knife is not available, then a razor knife will do.

FIGURE 1: *Cover Pieces*

Once you have just the shape you want, then proceed to cut fabric panels to cover it. Each face of the cushion should be covered with a separate piece of fabric with a few exceptions. The exceptions are for narrow lengths of fabric which can be used to completely encircle the edges of the cushion. Long, narrow strips of fabric can be easily handled and, thus, they make sense here.

---

*Ensolite M is not readily available in thicknesses greater than one inch, and it is very expensive relative to other open-celled foams. But I have found the one-inch thickness satisfactory, if not luxurious, and the expense can be justified, to a certain extent, when you take into account the flotation capabilities of the material. It is, indeed, the same material used in marine flotation jackets and survival gear.

**Airex is a relatively new closed cell foam from Switzerland. It is, like Ensolite M, waterproof and capable of being used as flotation material. But it is not so soft as Ensolite M. It makes up for this shortcoming by carrying a price tag about half that of Ensolite M. And Airex is available in thicknesses up to 2½ inches. All in all, this is the best choice for cushions.

Cut each piece of fabric with a ½-inch seam allowance where it will be sewn to other panels and with a 1½-inch allowance wherever a hem or a fastener is to be installed (but note below that some fastener systems require that special cloth assemblies be made to cover the the cushion side in question).

Each seam should be finished in the following manner:

1. First sew a length of braided Dacron cord in a similar length of vinyl or polyester binding. Do this with a zipper foot in your machine so that you can fold the binding over the cord and sew a line of straight stitches right along the cord holding it securely in place.

FIGURE 2: *The Piping Assembly*

2. Then place this "piping" between the two outside faces of the fabric panels as shown in Figure 3:

Place a row of stitches, again with the zipper foot in place, right along the cord as shown above. When the cover is turned right side out, the piping will be in place neatly over the seam.

FIGURE 3: *A Seaming Detail*

Sew together all parts of the cover. This will, of course, make of it a complete enclosure wrong side out. Cut a slit in the side along which you desire a closure system. This opening will be used to turn the cover right side out and will also provide the entry for the cushion.

Go ahead and turn the cover right side out. Now a means of covering and sealing the opening in the cover must be fashioned. This is the only mildly complicated task in making cushion covers.

First, make sure that the opening is large enough to permit the insertion of the cushion. Then enlarge that opening to a long rectangle roughly 5/8-inch wide. Seal the two edges with a hotknife or a soldering iron if the fabric that you are using is synthetic.

Next install the fabric strips along this opening that will enable the closure system to function. No matter what closure system you use, the fabric strips will be the same, although there are two manners in which they can be installed and the manner that you choose will depend upon the closure system that will be used. But more about that below. For now we can concern ourselves just with the fabric strips.

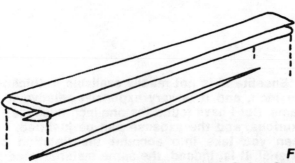

FIGURE 4
Rectangular Cover Opening And Tape Closure Strips

Start by cutting two strips of fabric two inches longer than the opening and three inches wide. Lay one strip over the fabric along one side of the opening and sew it in place with a row of straight stitches one inch from the opening's edge. Follow the same procedure with the other strip along the other side of the opening.

Then fold the two strips at the rows of stitches so that they overlap each other (see Figure 5). From this point on, the work will depend upon whether you are using a zipper or one of the other means of securing the opening. In Figure 5 I have shown a zipper installation in one series and Velcro in the other. In fact, the second series of illustrations applies to snap or common sense fasteners as well as to Velcro. In the case of a zipper, follow instructions under "1" below. If another type of closure is used, following instructions under "2."

FIGURE 5: *Closure Systems*

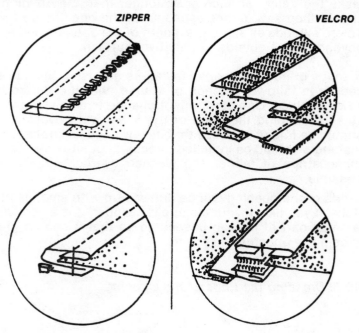

ZIPPER   VELCRO

1. Cut the strips at the ends of the opening so that they can be folded under to the inside of the cover (use a soldering iron or gun so that the cut edges will be sealed). Your zipper should be one inch longer than the opening. Undo the zipper and lay each half over the top sides of the strips so that the teeth face away from the opening. Keep the zipper tape's edge flush with the unsecured edge of the strip and sew the zipper halves to the tape with a straight stitch just 1/8-inch or so into the material. Then fold the strips back inside the cover with their attached zippers.

   Run a row of straight stitches down the entire length of the zipper on both sides of the opening roughly 1/2-inch from the zipper teeth so that a flap to cover the zipper teeth will be formed which will nevertheless allow free passage of the zipper slide. Stitch across the zipper tape at each end of the opening—lift the machine's presser foot and jump over the teeth.

2. Use 5/8-inch wide Velcro tapes in either a continuous length or in short lengths spaced six inches or so apart. Space snap or common sense fasteners on 6- to 12- inch centers. In either case, a 5/8-inch overlap of the two strips will be required. This can be provided by using 3/8-inch hems to finish the strip edges.

But, first, if Velcro is used, the tapes must be sewn to the upper face of the top tape and to the lower face of the tape underneath. Each Velcro tape should extend out over the edge of the strip to which it is attached by about ¼-inch. Run straight stitches all along the edges of the Velcro so that they are well attached to the strips. Then fold the tapes with the Velcro attached so that the two mating pieces are opposite one another as shown in Figure 5. A second row of straight stitches should be used to hold them here (study Figure 5). Make the Velcro an inch or so longer than the opening. You should then sew across each end of the opening so that the Velcro extends all along the length of the opening and slightly beyond on the outside of the cover surface.

If snaps or common sense fasteners are used, the same procedure is followed except, of course, that the Velcro is not sewn in place. One other minor change is also warranted. Instead of folding the edge of the lower strip over on top, it should be folded under so that its raw edge will not show. The fasteners should be installed directly opposite one another in these strips of fabric. The 5/8-inch overlap will make this possible.

The ends of the opening will be dressed up with small leather or fabric tabs, if you like. If your closure is a zipper, it is a good idea to leave a small part of the tab unsecured so that it can be grasped when closing or opening the cover.

FIGURE 6: *Dressing the Ends of the Opening*

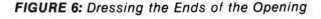

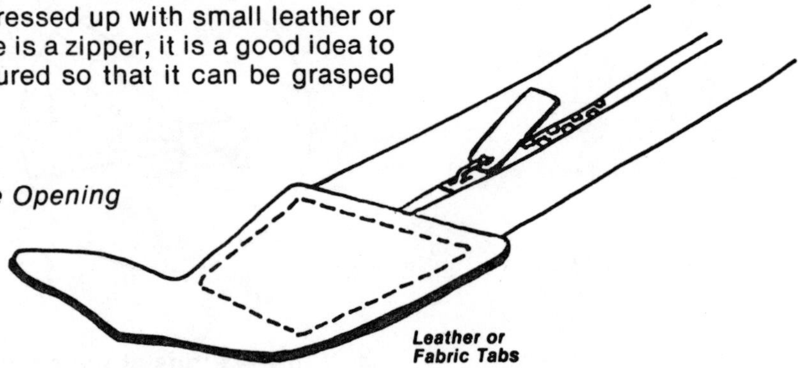

Leather or
Fabric Tabs

There are, of course, other means of constructing closures. I believe, however, that the system set forth above is most easily comprehended. But it would be a good idea to close this section by suggesting that a slightly neater installation will result if the fabric closure strips are cut large enough to actually make up the cover along the side in question.

If this method is used, leave the side of the cover into which the opening will be put completely open—don't even cut a piece for it. Then, when the other cover pieces are all assembled, cut two pieces—each two inches wider than half the width of the opening, plus the normal 1/2-inch seam allowances. Sew these strips in place along their long edges, using the piping technique described above. Leave the ends unsewn for now. Turn the cover right side out and finish the inner and overlapping edges just as you would in using the narrower strips described above (see "1" and "2" above). Finally, turn the cover inside out again and sew the ends of the opening strips in place.

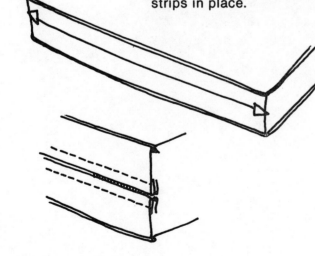

FIGURE 7: *A Modified Closure System Making Use of an Entire Side of the Cover*

6

Sail Covers

SAIL COVERS

Sail covers should be made of a fabric which "breathes" in order to prevent condensation. It should also, needless to say, be quite resistant to sunlight, stretch, and abrasion. Both polyester and acrylic fabrics fulfill these requirements, but certainly the best sail covers are made of the latter. The acrylics are more colorfast and tend to drape a bit better than the polyesters.

In this section, I will consider two types of sail covers. Those placed over sails furled on booms will be considered first. Then I will turn to the problem of covering self-furling sails.

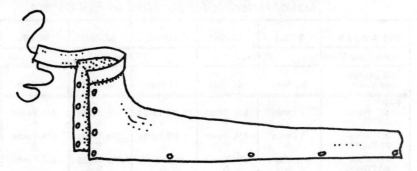

Boom Sail Covers

There are only a few materials, other than fabric, necessary for boom sail covers: thread, leather, fasteners, tie line, and binding (if desired). The **thread** should be V-60 or V-92 polyester. White is generally used even with colored fabric although colored thread is available if one is willing to put up with the handling problems caused by its increased brittleness and its lesser strength.

Machine stitching in sail covers is primarily straight. Make the stitches as long as possible. Some cover fabrics tend to "needle pucker" so the fewer times your needle penetrates the cloth the better the seam will look.

Leather is used for chafe protection wherever necessary. It is also a means by which handwork can be attractively covered.

There are several **fasteners** used for sail covers. My favorites are "twist-lock fasteners" (also called "common sense fasteners" and sometimes "carriage fasteners"). Some prefer to install hooks on one side of the cover so that it can be laced in place with a length of light line. Velcro tapes and zippers are also sometimes employed. Whatever fastening system you choose, be sure that it is secure and quick—these are the two requisites of a properly fastened cover.

Any **tie lines** should be polyester since it resists sunlight so much better than nylon or any natural fiber. I like to use #505 polyester leech line for the mast boot ties in my sail covers.

Binding is an option. If there is not enough cloth to form proper hems along the edges of the cover, it can be used to protect those edges and to keep the material from raveling. But even if you are able to fashion proper hems, the binding can add an attractive finishing touch to the cover. I like to use a braided acrylic binding, because it stays soft and flexible, but some sailmakers use a vinyl-coated nylon material that looks very nice.

We produce boom sail cover kits in six sizes at Sailrite. Needless to say, these kits perfectly match the needs of only a few boats. But the covers can easily be made too large and then cut to proper shape using the sail in question in its normally furled position as a form. This is the procedure that I recommend here. Even experienced sailmakers often standardize their cutting procedures as outlined below—it reduces labor requirements to a minimum, even though a bit of fabric will be wasted (much of this can be used for small cover projects).

Materials appropriate for the six sail cover sizes that we will consider are presented in Table 1.

TABLE 1
List of Materials for Six Sizes of Sail Covers

Sail Cover Kit	SC-04L	SC-04H	SC-05L	SC-05H	SC-06L	SC-06H
Boom Less Than	10 Feet		13 Feet		16 Feet	
Luff Length Less Than	32 Feet	49 Feet	33 Feet	52 Feet	34 Feet	55 Feet
FABRIC 40" Wide PATTERN	4 Yards A	5⅓ Yards B	5 1/6 Yards A	6⅔ Yards B	6⅓ Yards A	8½ Yards B
36" Wide PATTERN	4 Yards A	5⅓ Yards B	5 1/6 Yards A	6⅔ Yards B	6⅓ Yards A	8½ Yards B
31" Wide PATTERN	5½ Yards B	6½ Yards B	6⅔ Yards B	7⅔ Yards. B	8½ Yards B	19½ Yards B
V-69 Polyester Thread (1-oz. Tube)	6 Tubes	8 Tubes	8 Tubes	10 Tubes	10 Tubes	12 Tubes
#505 Leech Line	4 Feet	4 Feet	5 Feet	6 Feet	6 Feet	7 Feet
Leather	½ sq. ft.	½ sq. ft.	½ sq. ft.	½ sq. ft.	1 sq. ft.	1 sq. ft.
Common Sense Fasteners	10	10	12	12	18	18
Acrylic Binding	13 Yards	13 Yards	15 Yards	15 Yards	19 Yards	19 Yards

Note that there are three widths of fabric listed. These are more or less standard canvas widths. The 31-inch material is woven to provide the least waste in awning work. The greatest variety of colors and patterns will be found in material of this width. The 36-inch and 40-inch widths are especially woven for the marine industry—they cut work and waste in building sail covers to a minimum. But there are only a few solid colors available in that width. (Blue, yellow, and white are currently available in acrylic; blue, green, tan, brown, and drab in polyester.)

Begin by outlining the cover parts on the length of cloth. Figure 1 illustrates the proper panel layout for booms that are less than 10 feet. Figure 2 illustrates the layout for booms to 13 feet. And Figure 3 illustrates the layout for booms to 16 feet. Depending upon the width of the material with which you are working and the size of the sail that you are covering, you will want to use either Pattern A or Pattern B in each figure. Each Pattern B is distinguished by two extra pieces of fabric to increase the height of the cover up the mast—we call those pieces "top portions" in what follows. Study the appropriate drawing in Figures 1, 2, or 3 until you understand the use of each part of the cover.

FIGURE 1
The 10-Foot Boom Sail Cover Pattern

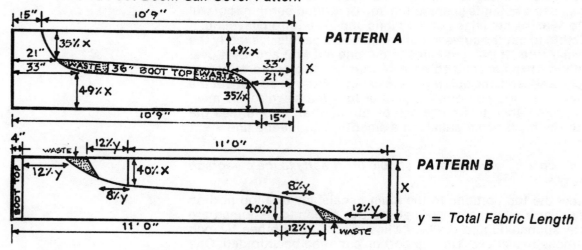

PATTERN A

PATTERN B

y = Total Fabric Length

FIGURE 2
The 13-Foot Boom Sail Cover Pattern

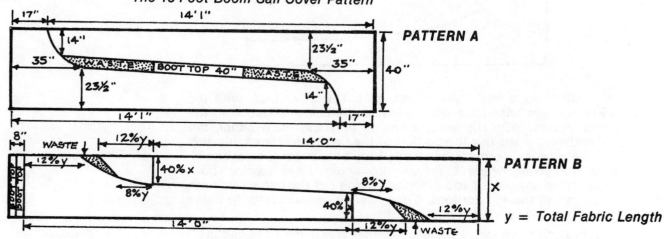

PATTERN A

PATTERN B

y = Total Fabric Length

FIGURE 3
The 16-Foot Boom Sail Cover Pattern

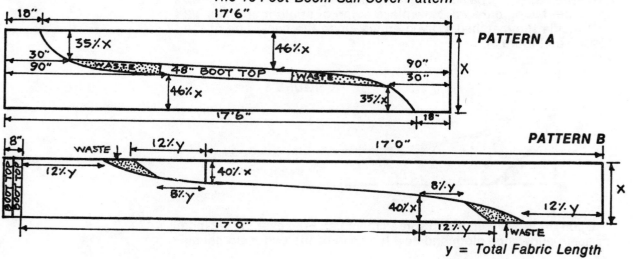

PATTERN A

PATTERN B

y = Total Fabric Length

Cut out the cover parts. This can be done with an ordinary scissors since all edges will be either hemmed or bound. But, if possible, use a hotknife (a soldering iron or a wood burning tool will work) to seal the cut edges of the fabric and keep it from raveling. It is desirable to cut the curve in both main boom panels in exactly the same way. Thus, it is a good idea to cut one out first and lay it over the outline of the second to be sure that the two conform before cutting the second one out. If you are using Pattern B, do not cut the curve into the "top portions" until after they are sewn to the main boom panels—then this curve can be cut so that it continues the curve of the main boom panels in a smooth, continuous line.

(Those working with Pattern A should go directly to the paragraph after next.)

To sew the top portions to the main panels, lay one top portion directly over a main panel so that the two edges to be joined are perfectly aligned (Figure 4). Place a line of straight stitches 1/2 inch inside those two edges. The top portion can then be unfolded. One

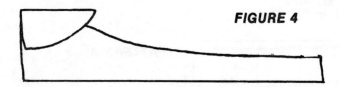

FIGURE 4

side will show a neat "stitchless" joint. The other side, with the 1/2-inch seam allowance will be inside the cover. Proceed in the same manner with the second top portion and main panel, but remember to place that top portion on the opposite side of this second main panel in order to be able to keep both seam allowances inside the cover where they will not show. After sewing both assemblies, lay one on top of the other and cut the curve into both aft edges of the top portions. From now on, we will refer to these assemblies as "main boom panels."

Join both main boom panels together down their "backbone." Lay one panel directly over the other. The surfaces now facing outward will be on the inside of the cover when we are done, so, if you are using *Pattern B*, be sure that the seam allowances from the step above are facing outward. Now place a line of straight stitches 1/2 inch inside the matched, curved edges along the backbone of the cover (see Figure 5).

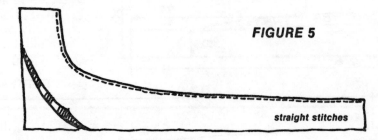

FIGURE 5

straight stitches

Open the sewn panels and spread them flat. Fold over the 1/2 inch of seam allowance cloth and sew it to one of the two main panels

FIGURE 6

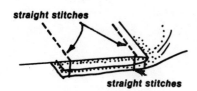

straight stitches

straight stitches

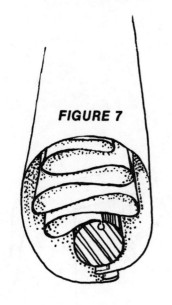

FIGURE 7

with two lines of straight stitches. The resulting seam will have a cross section like that represented in Figure 6.

Place the cover over the sail furled in the normal way on the boom. The cover should encircle the boom and overlap itself approximately two inches with at least a one inch further allowance for hems (Figure 7). The overlap at the leading edge of the mast should also be two inches. The same overlap should be present at the end of the boom.

If the cover is too short for the boom, but there is extra cloth encircling the mast, sew the aft part of the opening around the mast shut so that the whole cover moves aft. This will create a flat extension for the cover behind the mast. Some prefer this anyway since it provides a pocket for the headboard.

sew this area
if more cover length
is needed

If the cover is too small, try to devise a method of furling the sail which results in a better distributed bundle of fabric and which thus provides for the needed overlap.

You will probably have excess cloth at all edges (Figure 8). If the excess is less than three inches, fold the extra cloth under and inside the cover. Press the folded edge with a heavy, flat object to provide a clear sewing guide—do not use heat. Run a row of straight stitches right along the folded edge. Then run a second row of stitches 3/4 inch or so inside that edge (this row of stitches can be less than 1/2 inch inside the edge if there is little cloth available for a hem).

excess can be
folded under,
trimmed away, or
left in place

second stitch

FIGURE 8

first stitch

If the cover is over three inches too big anywhere, use your soldering gun or wood burning tool to trim it down to a hemmable size. Then proceed as above to install the hem.

If there is no extra cloth for a hem or if the extra cloth tapers to nothingness, do not fret. All edges can be bound with white acrylic braid or a white vinyl coated Dacron tape to provide needed protection. I prefer the former here because it is more easily worked around curves. To install this binding braid, simply fold it in half and slip it over the edges of the cover. Sew it down with a zigzag stitch.

Start with the aft end of the cover. You may want to sew this end closed if the boom rests on a crutch. Otherwise, the topping lift will be secured to the end of the boom and the end of the cover will have to be open to slip around it. If so, bind or hem these open edges. Then bind or hem the long edges along the bottom of the cover. Proceed in the same fashion with the forward facing edges of the mast boot.

Also bind or hem all four edges of the boot top strip (see Figure 9). Of course, if your pattern shows the boot top in two pieces, it will first be necessary to join them together end-to-end. Use the same connecting seam used in all previous work. The boot top should be long enough to circle the mast roughly 1½ times. It need be no longer than this. If it is, simply cut it down.

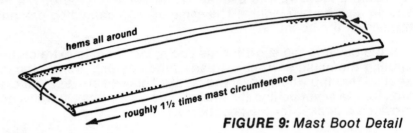

hems all around

roughly 1½ times mast circumference

FIGURE 9: *Mast Boot Detail*

Then sew the boot top to the top of the main panel. Overlap the two about 3/4 inch with the boot strip outside and run two straight stitches over the overlap about 1/2 inch apart (Figure 10).

Now sew a length of Dacron line across the middle of the boot top strip at or near its free end. This line will be used to tie the boot off around the mast, making it weather tight (Figure 11).

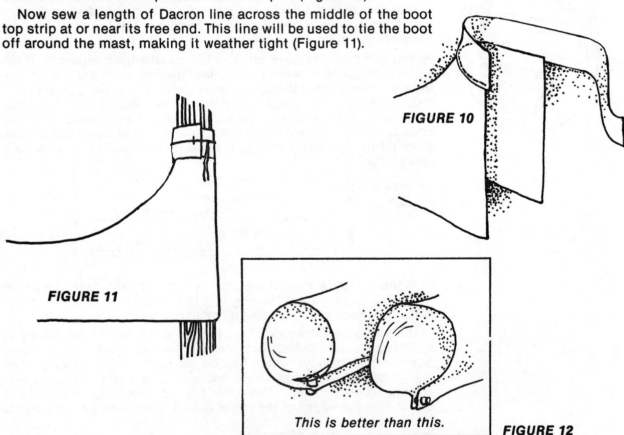

FIGURE 10

FIGURE 11

This is better than this.

FIGURE 12

The cover should now be placed over the furled sail again and the fastening system installed. Perhaps the most common fastener for sail covers is the common sense or "twist lock" fastener. I like to install these so that the cloth laps over itself rather than mating inside surface to inside surface (see Figure 12). The lapped closure puts stress on the fasteners in sheer, and it means that the finished side of the cover will be on the outside of the cover.

To install twist-lock fasteners, the only tool required is a small knife. Press the fastener stud or socket into the cloth where it is to be placed so that its prongs leave slight indentations. (It helps to place the fabric on a phone directory or some fairly yielding surface.) Make a small slit in the cloth with the point of your knife over these indentations. With synthetic cloth it is a good idea to heat the knife blade before making the slit so that it will be well sealed. Insert the prongs of the stud or socket through these slits and place an appropriate backing plate inside them on the other side of the cloth. Then bend the prongs over onto the backing plate with a pair of pliers.

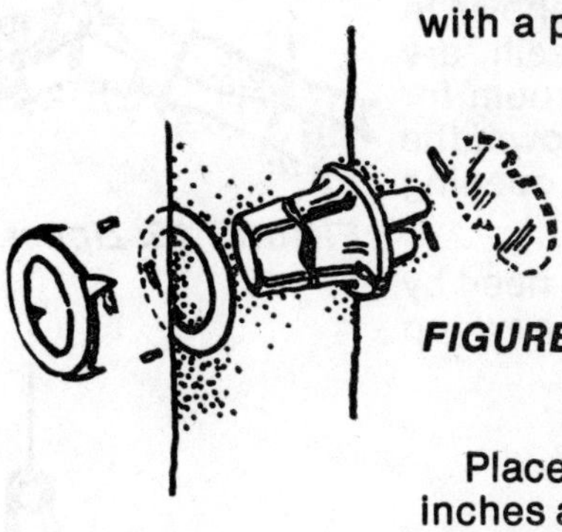

FIGURE 13: Twist-lock Fastener

Place fasteners at all corners of the cover and also from 20 to 38 inches apart between the corners to assure that the wind will not lift an edge and cause it to flap.

There are other fastening systems that can be used. Velcro straps, for example, are popular. One-inch wide Velcro loop tape roughly 3 inches long is sewn on the outside of one side of the cover. A hook tape 3 inches long is sewn on the inside of the opposite side. The cover can then be lapped over itself and secured. The Velcro system is fast and easy, but it is not so dependable as common sense fasteners.

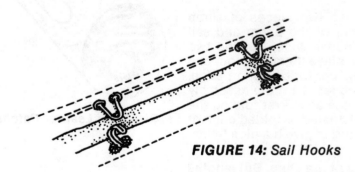

FIGURE 14: Sail Hooks

Sail hooks are also commonly used (Figure 14). These are generally sewn or riveted to the outside of one side of the cover. On the opposite side a 1/4-inch Dacron line is inserted in the hem of the cover (the hems may have to be enlarged). The line should exit the hem and reenter through two #1 spur grommets directly opposite each sail hook. Sew this line into its hem at the aft end of the cover and tie its other end round the mast after hooking all loops and pulling it tight. A similar closure system can be employed along the forward side of the mast.

If you prefer a hooked-on cover and do not have sufficient hem, the grommets can be installed as above and the line can be left exposed all along its length.

A simple alternative to all the above hardware is a number of webbing strips sewn to opposite sides of the cover with "Box-X" stitches. These can be tied together with square knots.

Finally, a nice way to close the forward side of the cover along the mast is to use a finished-length zipper (Figure 15). To install a zipper along the front opening of the sail cover (or anywhere else, for that matter), simply finish the opening with hems so that the two edges just meet (there need be no overlap). Then sew the zipper tape in place along each side with two rows of straight stitches as shown in Figure 15. Note that the stitches nearest the zipper teeth are placed roughly 3/16 inch away from those teeth to allow room for passage of the zipper slider. If the zipper is installed as shown, the teeth will be completely covered by flaps of cloth when the opening is zipped closed.

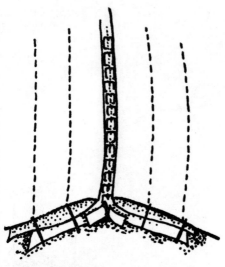

FIGURE 15: *Zipper Installation*

Finished zippers can be shortened to just the length you need by cutting off their tops. Melt two or three of the teeth at the new top end of the zipper to keep the slider from coming off.

A small piece of pearl grey leather can be used to protect edges which may be subjected to chafing, such as in the area around the topping lift. It can also be used to build in leather patches near the center of the cover to provide protection for exit slits provided for a halyard sling (see Figure 16). Most machines are capable of sewing this leather—try that first. If the machine balks, simply sew the leather in place with a needle and seven or eight strands of Dacron thread or some sail twine.

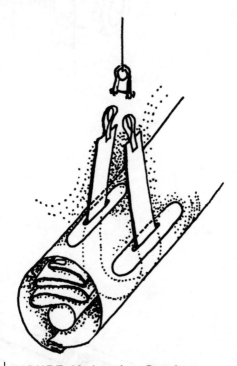

To make a halyard sling (Figure 17), use two pieces of scrap roughly 1½ times as long as the diameter of the boom and sail where it will be used and three or four inches wide. Cut the two pieces so that they are the same size. Then place them together one on top of the other and sew all around, except for one short edge, with a straight stitch 1/2 inch from their edges. Turn the assembly inside out and sew down the remaining edge after first folding the raw edges inside. Place this last stitch very near the folded edge of the fabric and continue it all around the sling to give it a nice finished appearance.

FIGURE 16: *Leather Patches*

Grommets should be placed in the ends of the sling. But lengths of fabric (six or seven inches) folded several times lengthwise and sewn to the ends to form loops will serve quite well also. The halyard can be shackled to these grommets or loops to keep it from banging the mast or chafing against the rigging.

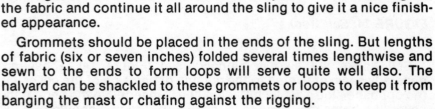

FIGURE 17: *Halyard Sling*

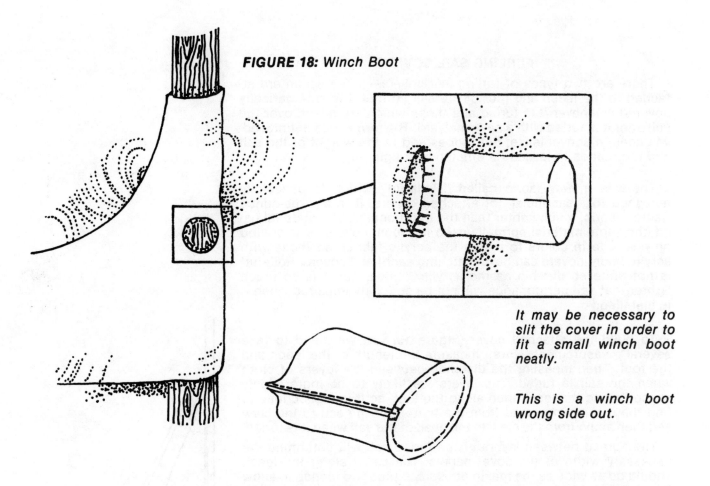

FIGURE 18: *Winch Boot*

It may be necessary to slit the cover in order to fit a small winch boot neatly.

This is a winch boot wrong side out.

Often there will be winches on the mast in the way of the cover. You can merely allow enough extra cloth when trimming to cover them "tent" fashion. A neater appearance, however, will result if a hole is cut in the cover to allow the winch to protrude and a special winch cover (see Figure 18) is made up. To fashion this cover, cut from scrap cloth a rectangle equal in width to the height of the winch plus two inches and equal in length to the circumference of the hole which was cut in the cover plus four inches (to allow for closing the barrel and attaching it to the cover).

Form a barrel with this rectangle by folding it in half across its length and sewing across the two narrow ends with a row of straight stitches 1/2 inch inside the edges. Cut out a circular piece of cloth one inch in diameter greater than the diameter of the barrel just formed. I like to cut this circle out roughly and oversized. Then I pin it in place 1/2 inch inside one end of the barrel. It can then be sewn with a line of straight stitches directly over the row of pins. Any extra cloth in the circle can then be cut away.

Now turn the resulting winch pocket inside out and insert it in the cover hole. Pin it in place so that its bottom edge is flush with the opening in the cover. Run a line of stitches all around this opening 1/2 inch inside the two edges.

To prevent any of the raw edges from raveling, you may want to overcast them with a short zigzag stitch. Or you may even go so far as to install binding tape over them.

The sail cover is now complete. If you encounter any problems or have any suggestions, please let me know.

FURLING SAIL COVERS

There are two types of furling sail covers—those which are attached to the leech and foot of the sail so that it is automatically covered whenever it is furled and those which are raised over the sail after it is furled with a spare halyard. The former has definite advantages in convenience, but it does add to the weight of the sail and thus tends to lessen its efficiency in light air.

There is a new fabric called "Rollafurl" which is especially designed for "sacrificial" or attached covers. It is a three-ounce Dacron fabric, much lighter than the traditional acrylic material used (the same material normally used for boom covers). It is coated on one side in colors to match the acrylic fabrics so those with acrylic boom covers can have matching sacrificial covers. Rollafurl is not quite so durable as the acrylic fabrics, but it is so much lighter that sail performance will not be seriously impaired when it is installed.

To build the attached cover (Figure 19) you will need to take several measurements. First, measure the length of the leech and the foot. Then measure the distance between the layers of cloth when the sail is furled. The layers are likely to be more widely spaced along the leech than along the foot, so it is a good idea to find the maximum spread from the bottom of the sail to the clew and then again from the clew to the head of the sail when it is furled.

The spread between layers of the furled sail will determine the necessary width of the cover panels. The panel along the leech should be as wide as the maximum spread plus two inches to allow

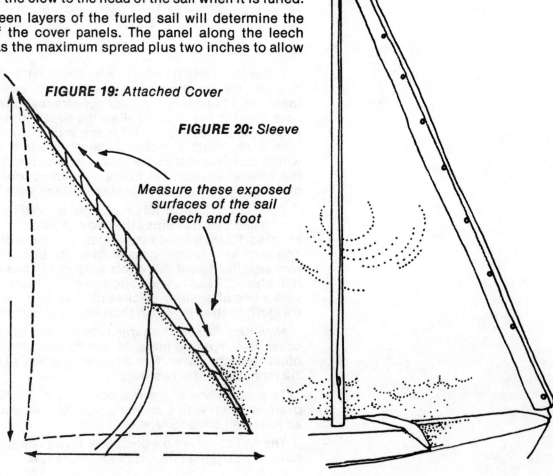

FIGURE 19: *Attached Cover*

FIGURE 20: *Sleeve*

Measure these exposed surfaces of the sail leech and foot

for hemming and inaccurate furling. The foot panel should be equal to the maximum spread there plus two inches also.

Cut sufficient lengths of both widths to cover the leech and the foot. Use your fabric as efficiently as possible. That is, don't hesitate to cut four strips from one panel width and sew them together end to end. Use the semi-flat felled stitch described in Figure 6 to make these connections. If the leech or the foot is sharply curved, you will want to make the connections so that these curves are nearly matched. The cover material will stretch a good deal more than the sail cloth, but the less you depend upon stretch to fit the curves of the sail edges, the better the cover will look. Be sure to join all lengths so that the raw seam edges will be down when the cover is placed on the sail.

Now fold over 1/2 inch of the cover material along both long edges. Fold the cloth over onto the seam allowance side of the cover. Sew the resulting hems in place with a single row of straight stitches right along the folded edge.

Then lay the cover over the edge of the sail to be covered. Be sure that the hems and the seam allowances are down against the sail so that the cover will have a neat appearance. Sew the cover to the sail with a row of zigzag stitches within 1/4 inch of the leech or foot edge of the sail all along the cover's length. You may want to experiment with pins or staples to secure the cover in place before sewing it.

You will certainly want to baste the other "inside" long edge of the cover to the sail. It is almost always necessary to secure that edge to the sail before sewing it. I like to use #465 transfer tape to accomplish this. If necessary, use pins or staples to supplement the tape (this will be especially helpful with acrylic cover cloth since the transfer tape does not stick to it well). As before you should use a single row of straight stitches about 1/4 inch from the cover edge.

Be sure to hem the cover at its ends as well as along its edges. This can only be done accurately after the cover has been sewn in place along its long edges.

In the tack and clew areas you may find that your machine balks at the thickness of the cloth. If so, get out your needle and a length of waxed sail twine and do it by hand with a simple flat stitch, that is, penetrate the material, move forward about 1/4 inch, penetrate it from the other side, and continue. Cut away the cover around the head, tack, and clew hardware. Once again, be sure to fold the cover under to form a hem at these points before sewing the material down.

That is all there is to it. If you have put the material on the right (as opposed to the "wrong") side of the sail, it will automatically provide a cover when the sail is furled.

The alternative to this attached cover is one that forms a sleeve which can be pulled over the furled sail with a spare halyard (Figure 20). These sleeves are really nothing more than long rectangles of cloth with a closure of some sort along the two long edges and grommets or fabric loops at the bottom and top.

The rectangle should have a width equal to the circumference of the sail at its largest plus six inches for hemming and clearance. The rectangle should be as long as the luff of the sail to be covered plus between two and six inches.

Hem the rectangle all around by folding over one inch of cloth at all edges. Run two rows of straight stitches along each hem. Place the first one right next to the folded edge—it will serve to hold the hem in place during the next pass through the machine and to keep it from shifting.

The closure device used will depend upon personal preference. I like to use common sense fasteners (twist lock fasteners) on 28-inch centers (see boom sail cover instructions for installation). I have seen a few covers with zipper closures. Although somewhat expensive, the zipper does provide a continuous and quite secure closing. Be sure that the zipper starts at the end of the cover that will be up near the top of the mast. It can then be started and closed while the cover is being raised. To install the zipper, just attach one zipper tape to the underside of each long cover edge with two rows of straight stitches. The most finished appearance will result if you allow the cover edge to extend over one half of the width of the zipper teeth although your stitches must, of course, be placed back away from the teeth to allow passage of the zipper slide.

There must be a means of attaching the halyard to the cover, and there should also be an attachment point for a line which can be used to hold the cover down over the sail. These attachment points can be #3 grommets, or they can be simple six-inch loops of fabric folded three times along their length and secured to the ends of the cover to provide loops.

I like to use a length of binding tape around the top and bottom of my cover sleeves. This helps prevent chafe damage and, at the same time, improves the appearance of the cover.

Your furling cover is now complete. If you use it faithfully, the life of your sail will be more than doubled. It is a good investment.

7

Small Covers

SMALL COVERS

This section concerns the numerous small covers which are so handy and useful on board a boat. They are surprisingly easy to make and often can be made up of scraps left over from larger projects. I cannot possibly describe all the varieties of small covers here, but, by considering in detail the construction of four distinct types, the basic principles will be conveyed and, with this background, you should be able to conceive and build almost any other small cover that might be needed. I want to consider, first, winch covers. Then we will turn to binnacle and wheel covers, then tiller covers, and, finally, outboard covers.

Winch Cover Instructions

The winch covers described here consist of an outer skirt and an inner "choker" which secures the cover neatly in place. Winch covers are generally made of the same fabric as the sail cover. Thus, it is often possible to build all that are needed with scraps left over from the sail cover. The only other materials needed will be V-69 thread, a short length of 1/4-inch shock cord or elastic, and a short length of binding tape. Follow the step-by-step instructions below.

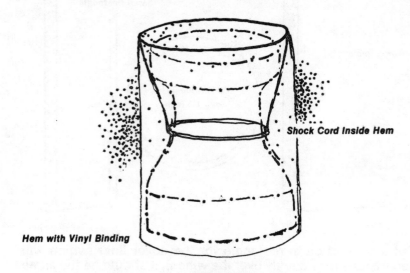

Shock Cord Inside Hem

Hem with Vinyl Binding

FIGURE 1
Detail of the Finished Winch Cover

1. Cut a rectangle of cloth to make the outside surface of the cover. Its length should equal the diameter of the winch base plus 1½ inches. Its width will be the height of the winch plus two 3/4-inch seam allowances.

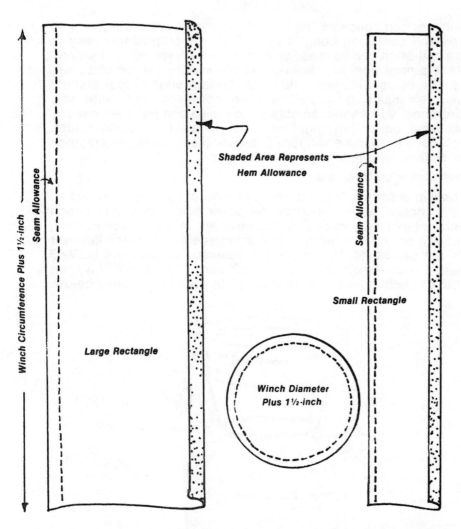

FIGURE 2: Winch Cover Parts

Winch Circumference Plus 1½-inch

Seam Allowance

Shaded Area Represents Hem Allowance

Seam Allowance

Small Rectangle

Large Rectangle

Winch Diameter Plus 1½-inch

2. Cut a second cloth rectangle for the cover liner (which will secure the cover snugly over the winch). It should be the same length as the first rectangle but just half as wide.

3. Place 3/4-inch hems along one long edge of both rectangles. Crease the hem fold carefully first with a heavy, flat object (such as an iron — but don't use heat). With the larger rectangle run two rows of stitches along the folded hem. The first should be placed very near the folded edge. Then place the second near the other edge of the hem allowance. The hem in the smaller rectangle will form a sleeve into which shock cord will be inserted so it should be sewn with only one row of stitches and that should be along the inner edge (i.e., not the folded edge) of the hem.

FIGURE 3: *Hem Detail*

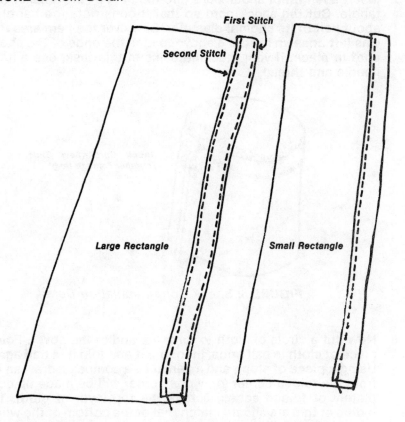

First Stitch

Second Stitch

Large Rectangle

Small Rectangle

4. Fold each rectangle in half across its width with the hem outside. Sew the short ends together with a row of straight stitches 3/4-inch inside the open, narrow, end. Do not sew over the hem of the small rectangle—this will leave an opening for the insertion of an elastic cord.

Sew Across the Ends

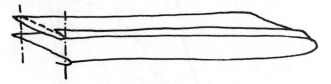

FIGURE 4: *Sewing the Winch Cover Barrels*

5. Insert a length of shock cord into the hem of the smaller rec-
    tangle. Cut the shock cord so that it constricts the barrel to
    about half of its original diameter. Sew over the hem area that
    was left unsewn in step 4 above to lock the ends of the shock
    cord in place. If your machine balks at this task, use a hand
    needle and thread.

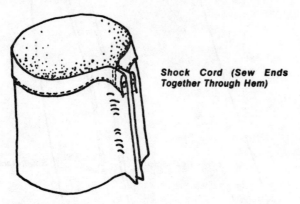

Shock Cord (Sew Ends Together Through Hem)

FIGURE 5: *Shock Cord Installation Detail*

6. Now cut a circle of cloth to form the end of the cover. Fold a
    piece of cloth in half once, then turn it and fold it in half again.
    Using a piece of string and a pencil as a compass, draw an arc
    from the folded corner (only one corner will be made up com-
    pletely of folded edges) across the top layer of cloth. The
    radius of this arc should match that of the bottom of the winch
    plus 3/4-inch for the seam allowance. Cut on this arc, unfold
    the material, and you should have a nearly perfect circle.

FIGURE 6: *Quarter Folded End Blank*

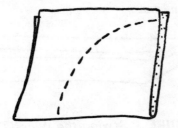

7. Fit the three pieces together now. All hems should be outside. Slide the small barrel over the larger one until the ends without hems are flush. Fit the circle into this opening and pin or staple it in place so that its outer edge is flush with the others. Run a row of straight stitches 3/4-inch inside these three flush edges.

FIGURE 7
*Installing the End Circle
in the Winch Cover Barrels*

8. Turn your cover inside out. It is now finished unless you desire a vinyl or Orlon binding tape which can be run all around the bottom edge to protect it from chafe. Fold the binding in half and sandwich the edge with it. Use the zigzag stitch, if possible, to secure it.

FIGURE 8
A Binding Installation

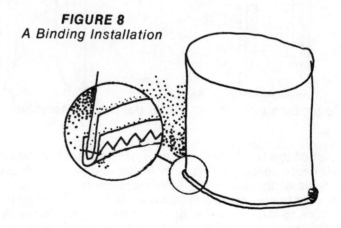

Binnacle and Wheel Covers

Once again, binnacle and wheel covers are generally made of the same material as the sail cover. In addition to fabric, you will need V-69 thread and a length of binding.

There will be a good deal of variety in the shape of wheels and binnacles, but these instructions will be complete and sufficient for most of them. Even if some modification proves necessary, you will find all the essential principles of construction here. Simply apply them as necessary to meet your particular requirements.

1. Measure the wheel diameter (A).

2. Measure the distance from the deck to the top of the wheel (B).

3. Cut out a piece of cloth as wide as the wheel diameter plus 1½ inches and as long as the height of the top of the wheel off the deck plus 1½ inches. Cut the top of this rectangular piece of cloth with a radius equal to that of the wheel plus 3/4-inch.

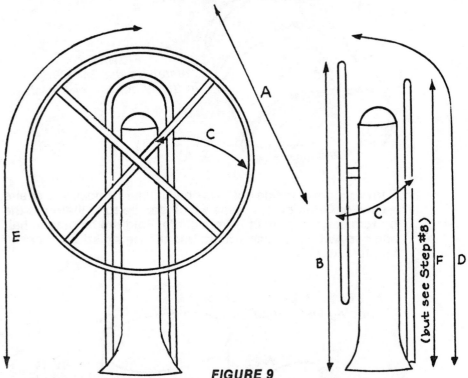

FIGURE 9
Controlling Dimensions for Wheel Cover Assemblies

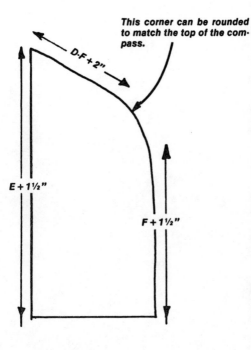

4. At the level of the horizontal diagonal of the wheel, measure from the forward center of the binnacle (around any guardrails) to the outside of the wheel (C). Also measure from the top of the wheel over the binnacle and down to the deck (D). Measure from the deck to the top center of the wheel around its arc (E). And, finally, measure from the deck to the binnacle guardrail top (F)—but see Step 8 for a possible modification if the rail is very much higher than the binnacle itself.

5. Cut two pieces of cloth with the following dimensions:

FIGURE 10
Side Panels (Two Required)

6. Put one of the pieces of cloth cut in Step 5 directly over the other and sew them together with a straight stitch 3/4-inch inside edges D and F.

7. Next sew the piece cut in Step 3 to this assembly along edges E. Start sewing at the top of the radiused section and work down both sides E with your stitch. Once again, keep the straight stitch 3/4-inch inside the two edges. Make sure that those edges are "outside." When finished, turn the resulting bag inside out to expose neat seams.

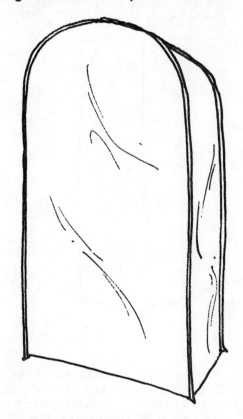

FIGURE 11
The Cover Inside-Out

8. Test fit the cover. If there is a binnacle guardrail that rises far above the compass, you may want to slit the material so that the rail protrudes through and allows the cover to settle down over the wheel. Hem the bottom of the cover by folding under excess cloth—secure the hem with two rows of straight stitches. Add a binding tape to further protect the bottom edge of the cover, if desired.

9. If a binnacle guardrail cover is needed because of a slit cut in Step 8, fashion it out of two pieces of cloth. Cut them to fit the front and back of the exposed rail and add three inches for hem allowance and rail thickness. Sew them one on top of the other with straight stitches 3/4-inch inside their top and side edges (leave the bottom open).

Turn the assembly right side out and sew it to the main wheel cover. Be sure to accomplish this in such a fashion that the seam allowance remains on the inside of the cover. Use pins or staples to baste it in place before using a straight stitch with a 3/4-inch seam allowance.

FIGURE 12
The Complete Wheel and Binnacle Cover

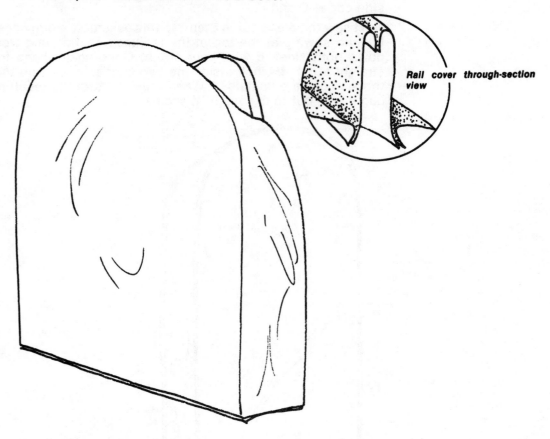

Rail cover through-section view

Tiller Covers

Tiller covers are also generally made of cloth matching the sail cover. They are made up by cutting two pieces of cloth, using the side of the tiller as a pattern. Leave two to three inches of extra cloth all around. The thicker the tiller the greater the allowance must be. But tiller covers should not fit tightly, so be generous in your allowance.

1. If it is possible to slide the cover on the tiller and drop its open end down over the rudder or the rudder post, you can use the "pocket style" as shown in Figure 13.

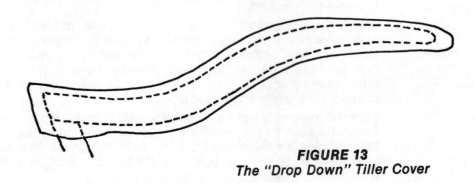

FIGURE 13
The "Drop Down" Tiller Cover

2. Or an elastic band can be used to strap the cover over the rudder or the rudder post.

3. If there is no rudder or rudder post to hook onto, consider a simple shock cord or elastic friction band in the open end of the cover.

4. Or use a drawstring to snug the cover down around the tiller.

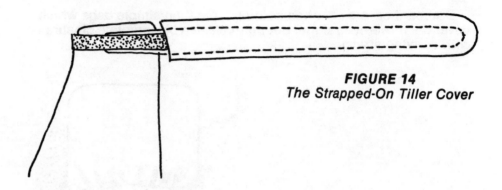

FIGURE 14
The Strapped-On Tiller Cover

5. Any of the methods above can be complemented by snap-fasteners, Velcro, or even twist-lock fasteners used in a surface to cloth configuration. That will insure that the cover will not come off accidentally.

To build the cover, simply put the two pieces of fabric cut above on top of one another and run a row of straight stitches all around them 3/4-inch inside the two edges except for the opening required for installation.

Then turn the cover inside out. A broom handle may be handy in accomplishing that.

Finally, finish the opening with a hem or a sleeve. You may want to use binding tape in addition to or instead of a hem. If a drawstring is desired, finish the sleeve around the opening after first folding down triangular tabs and stitching them in place to provide reinforcement for the line exit points.

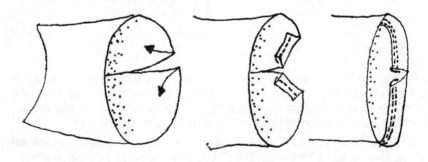

FIGURE 15
Rolled Tabs to Reinforce Drawstring Exit Points

Outboard Covers

Once again, outboard covers are generally built of the same material used for sail covers. In addition, depending upon the design, you will need some or all of the following: V-69 polyester thread, shock cord, #505 leech line for draw string, nylon or polypropylene webbing, #10 Delrin zipper, and 5/8-inch Velcro tapes.

Outboard covers are often nothing more than simple bags which cover the powerhead alone. But they can also be complete closures with carrying straps.

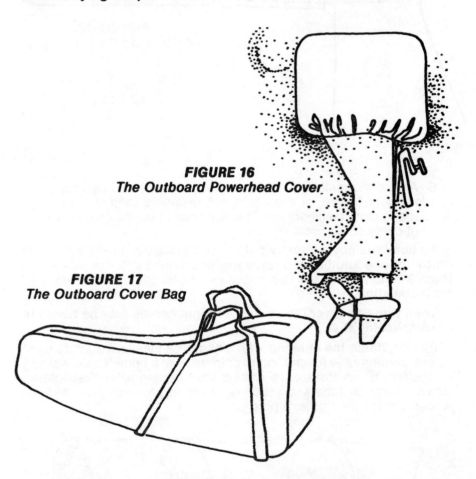

FIGURE 16
The Outboard Powerhead Cover

FIGURE 17
The Outboard Cover Bag

No matter how complex the cover that you are making, keep it large and loose-fitting so that it will be easier to put on and take off. Conceive of the outboard as a simple box with five or six sides, depending upon whether the cover is partial or complete.

Cut a piece of fabric for each facet of the box, allowing 3/4-inch all around as a seam allowance. Don't hesitate to round corners where appropriate and to narrow the panels in the way of the lower unit. But remember that a tight fit is not desirable, so don't get carried away.

Sew the panels together by laying adjacent ones on top of each other, outside surface to outside surface, and then by running a row of straight stitches 3/4-inch inside their edges. If the cover will be an open bag such as the one in Figure 16, you will be able to turn it right side out when done. All that remains of your task then is to fashion a sleeve through which a drawstring or a shock cord can be threaded. For the drawstring sleeve, fold over the corners of the exit points as illustrated in Figure 15 before making the sleeve itself. See the instructions above concerning winch covers for details concerning the installation of shock cord.

If your bag is a complete enclosure, it will be necessary to cut a slit in it before it can be turned right side out. But there must be an opening in any case in order to fit it over the outboard, so cut away. Use a scissors for the initial cut and then enlarge it to a long rectangle roughly 5/8 inch wide. Seal the two edges with a hot blade (a soldering iron or woodburning tool works fine).

Now turn the bag right side out through the opening, and install a #10 Delrin zipper or a Velcro closure to secure the opening.

To install either, start by cutting two strips of fabric two inches longer than the opening in the cover and three inches wide. Lay one strip over the fabric along one side of the opening and sew it in place with a row of straight stitches one inch from the opening's edge. Follow the same procedure with the other strip along the other side of the opening.

Then fold the two strips at the rows of stitches so that they overlap each other. From this point on, the work will depend upon whether you are using a zipper or Velcro tapes to close the opening.

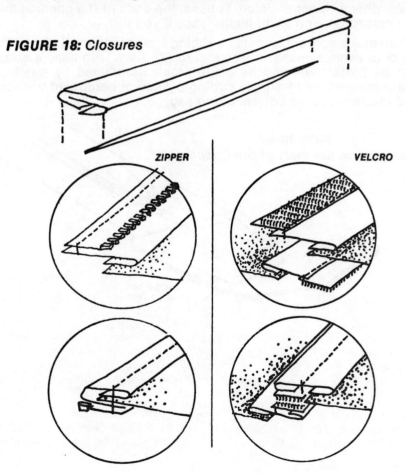

FIGURE 18: *Closures*

ZIPPER   VELCRO

Zipper

Cut the strips at the ends of the opening so that they can be folded under to the inside of the cover (use a soldering iron or gun so that the cut edges will be sealed). Your zipper should be one inch longer than the opening. Undo the zipper and lay each half over the top sides of the strips so that the teeth face away from the opening. Keep the zipper tape's edge flush with the unsecured edge of the strip and sew the zipper halves to the tape with a straight stitch just 1/8 inch or so into the material. Then fold the strips back inside the cover with their attached zippers.

Then run a row of straight stitches down the entire length of the zipper on both sides of the opening roughly 1/2 inch from the zipper teeth so that a flap to cover the zipper teeth will be formed which will nevertheless allow free passage of the zipper slide. Stitch across the zipper tape at each end of the opening—lift the machine's presser foot and jump over the teeth.

Velcro

Use 5/8-inch wide Velcro tapes. They will, of course, require a 5/8-inch overlap of the two strips. This can be provided by using 3/8-inch hems to finish the strip edges. But first the Velcro tapes can be sewn to each strip such that it is offset 1/4 inch. Run straight stitches all along the edges over the strip. Make the Velcro a couple of inches longer than the opening but sew across each end at the end of the opening so that the Velcro extends all along the length of the opening.

Whether a zipper or Velcro is used, the ends of the opening may be dressed up with small leather tabs if you like.

You may also want to install webbing straps that go all around the cover to serve as handles (see Figure 17). Bags with handle straps can be protected from the chafe problems caused by relatively sharp protrusions by simply cutting a piece of hardboard to shape and placing it in the bottom of the bag.

FIGURE 19
Dressing Up the Ends of the Opening

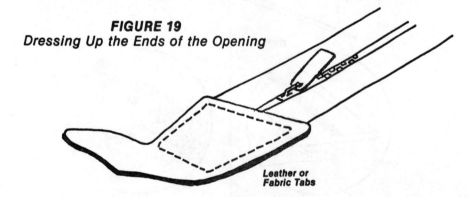

Leather or Fabric Tabs

8

Companionway Dodgers and Bimini Tops

COMPANIONWAY DODGERS AND BIMINI TOPS

Companionway dodgers and Bimini tops are, like awnings and enclosures, meant to provide protection. But they are meant to be used when underway. Thus, they must be even tougher than the fabrications that we considered in *Awnings and Enclosures*. This added strength is accomplished, in large part, by scaling them down and by using a metal frame comprised of two or more bows solidly secured to the cabin top or sides or to the cockpit coaming or the deck of the boat. This frame is constructed so that it can be folded down in really severe weather.

The two are distinguished by intended use and structure. Thus, the companionway dodger is intended to provide protection from wind and flying spray, while the Bimini top is meant to provide protection from the heat of the sun. These two distinctly different functions lead to quite different structures. The companionway dodger tends to be low and completely closed in front and on its sides. The Bimini top, on the other hand, tends to be high and quite open — there is often nothing more than a roof of fabric (Figures 1 and 2).

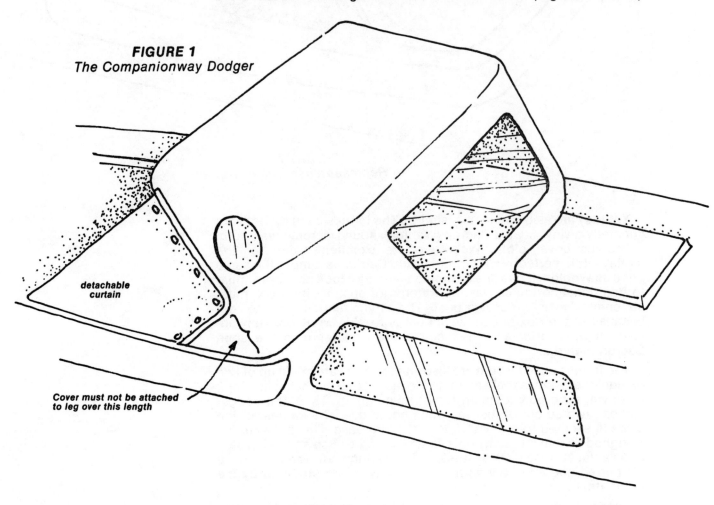

FIGURE 1
The Companionway Dodger

detachable curtain

Cover must not be attached to leg over this length

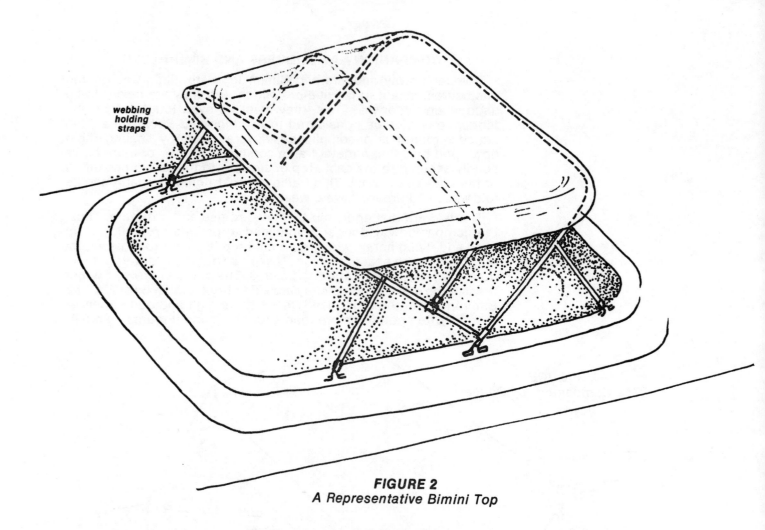

webbing
holding
straps

FIGURE 2
A Representative Bimini Top

Yet they are also remarkably similar. The fabrics used for both are generally a vinyl coated Dacron (Weblon), spun Dacron cover cloth, or acrylic cover cloth. Weblon offers excellent value for the money—it is perfectly waterproof. Spun Dacron is almost the same price as Weblon. It has one advantage—it has a look and feel similar to traditional cotton canvas. Its waterproof coating, however, must be renewed every other year or so. The acrylic fabrics look the best because of their extra bulk which tends to hide wrinkles. They are also slightly softer and their colors are brighter than the spun Dacron material.

The frames used by both are also similar. They are made up of two or more metal bows that are hinged to each other so that, when folded down, each bow rests on top of its neighbor. Thus, the dodger can be lowered out of the way when not in use. The longest of the bows is secured to the boat with a pivoting base. This base can be designed so that it mounts on a vertical surface such as a cabin side or on a flat surface such as the top of a coaming rail. The frames are supported upright either with adjustable webbing straps or by the fabric itself.

These frames should be cut so that the base width is 10 inches oversize. Then, when the legs are forced into place, an arc will be formed across the top of each bow. This arc strengthens the frame and keeps it from coming apart in use.

Frames up to 80 inches wide and 40 inches high can be con-·
structed from pre-bent aluminum tubing frame kits complete with
all necessary hardware. Each bow is made up of three separate
pieces of 7/8 inch OD hard annodized tubing. The two bent pieces

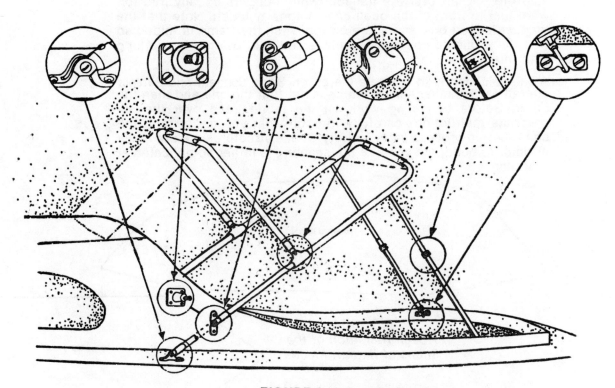

FIGURE 3: A Dodger Frame

are "swedged" (reduced in diameter) at their ends so they will slide
into the straight tubing that supports the roof fabric. The aluminum
tubing can easily be trimmed to proper size with an ordinary
hacksaw (Figure 3).

Larger frames are best constructed of stainless steel tubing cut
and welded together by a local welding shop. These steel frames
must be made up to fit the unique dimensions of each boat since
minor adjustments will not be possible without returning the whole
unit to the welding shop.

Whichever frame you use, make sure that it can be raised and
lowered under the boom. This requirement is necessary to permit
tacking the boom over the dodger or Bimini when underway. Also be
sure that the bows of the frame collapse one on top of the other so
that it can be folded down just in front of the hatch (or elsewhere)
when it is closed. Study the drawings here for frame details. Note
that the angle of the bows can be adjusted to provide just the height
and extension over the cockpit desired.

The first step in building a Bimini or a dodger is to either assemble the frame and mount it in position or to construct a mock-up of
taped-together clothes hangers. The former is possible with the pre-
bent aluminum frame. The latter is necessary when a pattern for a
stainless frame must be made up.

These Legs Must Be Equal

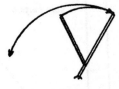

FIGURE 4
Frames Should Fold Flat

Support the bows in place temporarily with strips of masking tape. Adjust everything until you get just the protection and appearance desired. Be sure to check the lowered position of the frame—it must fold down neatly out of the way. Many Biminis are made to fold aft over the transom while dodgers usually fold forward just in front of the open companionway hatch. Note that the longest legged bow should be on top when the frame is folded so that the frame can be more easily raised and lowered by working with this bow alone.

The next step is to fabricate the cover. Since dodgers and Biminis are rather dissimilar here, I will consider first the one and then the other. Before beginning work on the fabric, read over the appropriate instructions carefully. Be sure that you understand the construction process in its entirety. These structures are not really difficult to build, but some of the seaming is rather complicated at first glance.

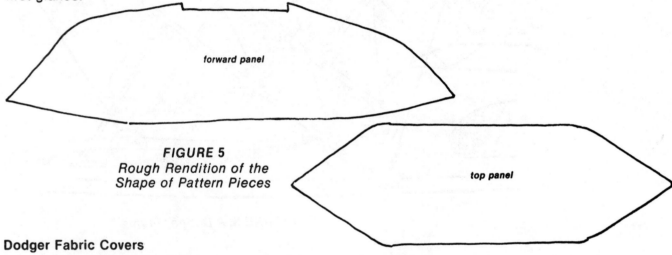

FIGURE 5
*Rough Rendition of the
Shape of Pattern Pieces*

Dodger Fabric Covers

In addition to cover fabric, you will require some or all of the following materials:

        Roughly eight feet of one-inch webbing
        Pattern paper or cloth
        V-92 or V-69 polyester thread
        Plastipane window material (.019 or .04-inch thick)
        Cloth-to-cloth fasteners
        Cloth-to-surface fasteners
        #465 transfer tape
        Velcro tape and Velcro contact cement
        Leather
        #10 Delrin zipper (optional)
        Aluminum boltrope extrusion (optional)
        ¼ inch Dacron boltrope (optional)

Using the pattern material, make up a full scale model of the finished cover. Begin by shaping the panel which stretches across the top of the frame. The curves along the leading and trailing edges of this "top panel" are critical so be sure that they are right. Use masking tape to secure the pattern material to the frames. Needless to say, if the pattern material is too narrow to provide the coverage needed, simply tape two or more pieces together.

In a companionway dodger, the top panel will have a shape similar to that shown in Figure 5.

Once the top panel pattern is cut, turn to the forward wall of the dodger. This is a difficult panel to fit because there must be provision for the sliding hatch and other protrusions on the deck. Before the fit can be made, one must decide where and how the leading edge of the dodger will be fastened.

One method of attachment is to use cloth to surface fasteners (snap or twist-lock). Twist-lock fasteners are often used when the sloping front surface of the fabric is brought right down to the flat cabin top — they will resist peel stress quite well. Snap fasteners can be used when there is a spray deflector moulded into the cabin top. This keeps all stress on the fasteners in shear. You may prefer to mount wedges of teak or mahogany along the deck if your boat does not have moulded spray rails. Such wedges are shown in Figure 6.

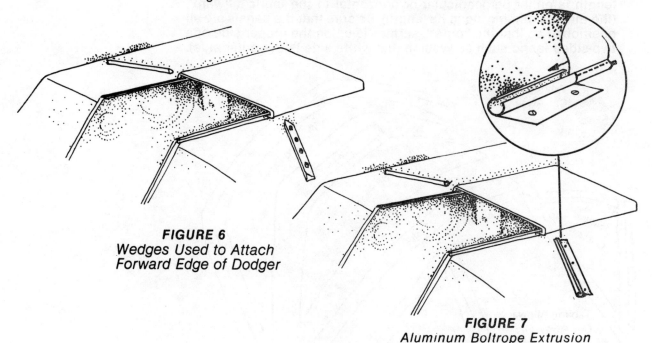

FIGURE 6
*Wedges Used to Attach
Forward Edge of Dodger*

FIGURE 7
*Aluminum Boltrope Extrusion
Used to Attach Forward Edge of Dodger*

A second way to secure the leading edge of the dodger is to fasten an aluminum boltrope extrusion to the boat. Then a ¼ inch boltrope can be sewn into the lower forward edge of the fabric and that can slide into the extrusion to form a nearly water-tight and extremely strong attatchment. Note that the extrusion can not be bent radically. If necessary, however, it can be cut into several short pieces. Carefully round the corners of the cut extrusion to prevent catching and tearing the fabric.

When you have decided upon the method for securing the leading edge of your cover and when the necessary hardware is in place, tape the forward panel pattern material in place as you trim it to fit. Needless to say, two or more pieces can be taped together if needed in order to make up a large enough panel.

Now fashion the two side curtain patterns. The side curtains will be snap fastened to a flap of fabric attached to the aft edge of the dodger and secured along the cockpit coaming. These curtains can thus be removed to allow air circulation on hot days at anchor. Their shape and the mode of their attachment to the hull will differ from boat to boat, but the matter should present little difficulty. Once again, tape the side curtain patterns in place.

Stand back and consider the shape of the dodger. Does it look good? If not, change the side curtains, the slope of the forward side or even the angle of the frame until it does. This may require new patterns, but it is better to make such adjustments now rather than going to the trouble of changing a finished dodger.

Remove the patterns from the frame. Be sure to mark the outer surface of each one. Lay them over the cover fabric so that their length is either perpendicular or horizontal to the fabric's "warp" (the threads running along its length). Be sure that the panels are all positioned so that the "outer" surface is up on the proper side of a two-sided fabric such as Weblon (the white side is the outer side).

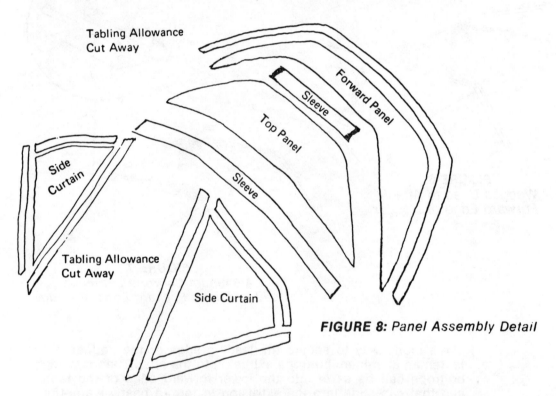

FIGURE 8: *Panel Assembly Detail*

There will be 13 distinct panels of cloth comprising your dodger as illustrated in Figure 8. Two are simply long strips used to create sleeves within which the frame is slipped. The shorter of these two is simply a rectangle 36" long and five inches wide. These "short sleeve" dimensions can be changed a good deal. Indeed, a zippered sleeve or a shorter sleeve is possible, or snap tabs or even simple webbing ties can be used instead of a sleeve. The only purpose of this short sleeve, after all, is to hold the forward bow in place. In spite of all these options, I will assume a short sleeve in what follows. The optional systems can be easily utilized once the principles of sleeve construction are understood.

The longer of the two sleeves is a duplicate of the last five inches of the aft edge of the top panel. Cut out the top panel, the forward panel, the two sleeves, and the side curtains, using your patterns as a guide. Allow 3/4-inch of extra cloth all around these panels as a seaming and hemming allowance. (The two sleeve strips do not require this extra cloth since it is included in the five-inch width specified.)

There are seven tabling strips* that will be used to trim and reinforce the curtain edges and the leading edge of the forward panel. Cut these strips three inches wide and exactly like the edges over which they will be placed. They will be reattached later to provide a finished edge all along the exposed parts of the dodger.

If two or more pieces of fabric have to be joined together to make a single panel, do so by placing one squarely over the other. If you are working with a two-sided fabric like Weblon, keep outside surfaces back to back. Stagger the panels about 5/8 inch. Sew them together with a row of straight stitches just inside the inner edge. Fold the stagger allowance over and sew it down with a second row of straight stitches along the allowance edge. Now unfold the top panel and spread the assembly flat. The 1/2-inch seam allowance will be folded underneath. This should be sewn in place with a third row of straight stitches on one side of the seam. A fourth row can be placed along the other side of the seam to make it a bit more secure. The resulting seam will look like Figure 9.

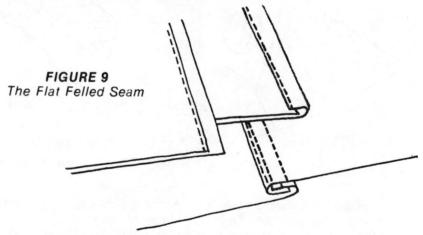

FIGURE 9
The Flat Felled Seam

This step-by-step flat felled seam construction is recommended for those with little experience. The use of #465 transfer tape at each step will further insure a neat and accurate seam. Those with more sewing experience, however, will be able to put the seam together in two passes through the machine. If you possess that experience, don't hesitate to use it.

---

*A tabling is a piece of cloth cut away from the edge of a panel, lifted up and placed over the new panel edge in the place of a hem. It is useful since it makes possible a perfect match of cloth grain in both sides of the hem—were the piece simply folded over, the grain would be reversed except where the panels were at right angles or parallel to the edge.

Be careful to join all panels so that the dodger will be symmetrical about its center axis—that is, the right side should have just as many seams in the same place as the left side does.

Now you can begin sewing the panels together. Figure 10 presents a cross section of the finished dodger through its center. Study this figure carefully so that the principle of construction is understood.

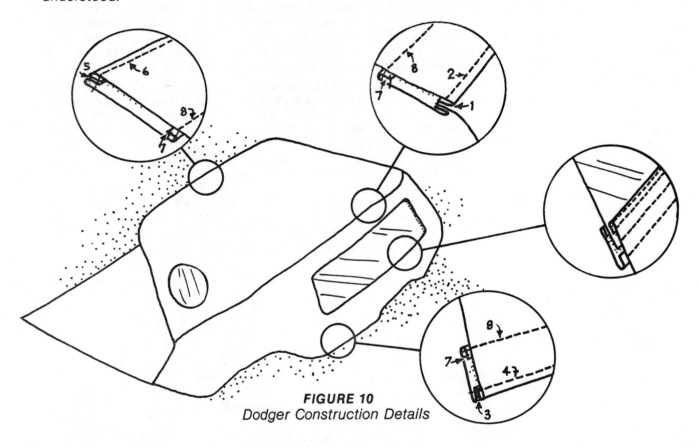

FIGURE 10
Dodger Construction Details

Place the forward panel with its inner side up on top of the outer side of the top panel. Over this place the short sleeve strip with its outer (i.e., upper) side up, but first put two 1/2-inch hems across the ends of this short sleeve strip by folding the outer side over against the outer side at each end. Center the hemmed short strip and match up the edges of all three panels over the forward edge of the top panel—the top panel will have to be forced back to permit the edges to match up (see Figure 11). Place a row of straight stitches 5/8 inch inside the matched edges from one corner of the top panel to the other (stitch #1 on Figure 10). I recommend that you either start your stitches in the center and work toward both ends or carefully baste all the edges together with staples or pins before sewing.

Unfold the foward panel and the short sleeve strip from the top of the top panel. The short sleeve should be folded all the way under the top panel—the forward panel will be folded out about 200 degrees (see Figure 10). Press the short sleeve up against the bottom of the top panel and sew it in this position with a row of stitches 1/4-inch from the first stitches and on the top panel side of those first stitches (stitch #2 on Figure 10).

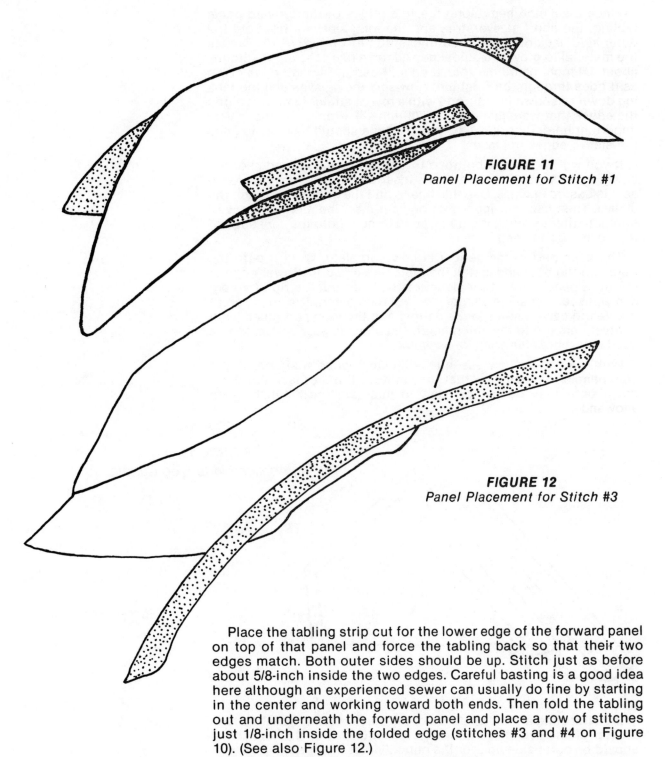

FIGURE 11
Panel Placement for Stitch #1

FIGURE 12
Panel Placement for Stitch #3

Place the tabling strip cut for the lower edge of the forward panel on top of that panel and force the tabling back so that their two edges match. Both outer sides should be up. Stitch just as before about 5/8-inch inside the two edges. Careful basting is a good idea here although an experienced sewer can usually do fine by starting in the center and working toward both ends. Then fold the tabling out and underneath the forward panel and place a row of stitches just 1/8-inch inside the folded edge (stitches #3 and #4 on Figure 10). (See also Figure 12.)

Next secure the long sleeve strip to the top panel. Place the strip outer side up on top of the outer side of the top panel. Match up the aft edges of both pieces and run a row of straight stitches about 5/8-inch inside them all along their length (stitch #5 on Figure 10). Fold the long strip down underneath the top panel and place a row of stitches 1/8-inch inside of the fold (stitch #6 on Figure 10).

Place a 5/8-inch hem along the free edges of the forward panel tabling, the short sleeve strip, and the long sleeve strip. Fold the outer side back on itself to do this (stitch #7 on Figure 10). Crease the material to provide a guideline and run a row of straight stitches about 1/4-inch inside the folded edge. Keep the folded edge down as it goes through the machine. Now sew the sleeves and the tabling down as shown in Figure 10 with a row of straight stitches along the edges that were just hemmed (stitch #8). Proper basting is very important here. Pins and #465 transfer tape should be used to keep the sleeve edges in place.

If you will be using a boltrope to secure the leading edge of the cover, there should be a small line inserted into the forward sleeve as it is basted in place. Use this line to pull the boltrope through the sleeve. Then use the zipper foot on your machine and run a row of straight stitches along the boltrope to force it onto the very edge of the cover and to keep it there.

The main part of the dodger is now complete. Work it onto the frame on the boat and install the fasteners along the lower edge of the front panel, so that the dodger is well sealed. A strip of Velcro can be used to seal the dodger over a sliding hatch. The hook part of the Velcro can be sewn to the dodger and the loop part glued (with contact cement) to the hatch itself. Needless to say, Velcro can be used anywhere else you like as well.

With the dodger now essentially finished, once again check the side panels to make sure that they still fit. If necessary, cut them down until they do but be sure to maintain the 3/4-inch seam allowance.

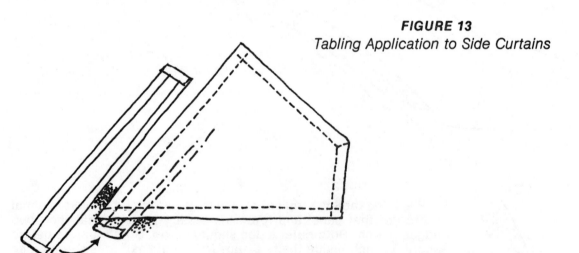

FIGURE 13
Tabling Application to Side Curtains

Install tabling around all edges of the curtains. Place each tabling on top of the proper curtain edge and flush with it. The tabling should be outer side up over the outer side of the curtain. Sew with a straight stitch 5/8 inch inside the flush edges. Do one edge at a time to completion. Put a hem along the ends and the unsecured long edges of the tabling strips by folding 5/8 inch of the outer side back upon itself and sewing it down. Then fold the tabling under onto the inner side of the curtain and secure this with a row of straight stitches along the inside edge of the tabling (see Figure 13).

Secure the side curtains to the dodger with a snap or twist-lock fastener. This can be done by simply locating the fasteners in the dodger itself just forward of the sleeve, but a better looking and stronger attachment will result if a flap of cloth is sewn to the dodger just forward of the sleeve (see Figure 14). The fasteners can be installed in the flap aft of the dodger frame.

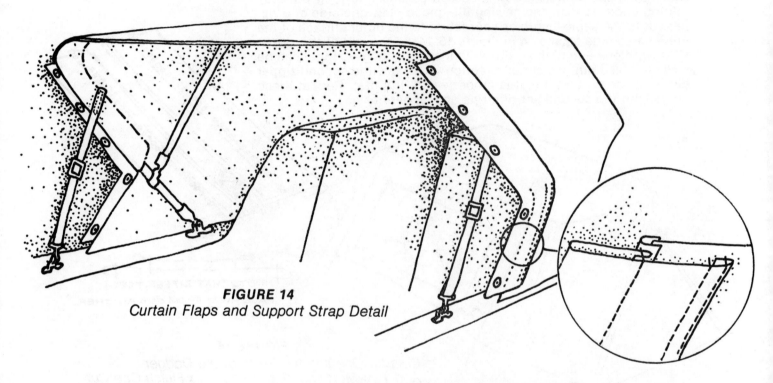

FIGURE 14
Curtain Flaps and Support Strap Detail

You may want to use snap or twist-lock fasteners to secure the curtains to the hull or you may want to use shock cord or rope to stretch them out. This makes it possible to quickly release the curtains if that is necessary to provide access for sheets or for the swing of winch handles.

If you want to keep the dodger up without the side curtains, it will be necessary to rig a strap to pull aft on the dodger frame (see Figure 14).

The final step of construction entails the installation of plastic windows. With the dodger up, attempt to determine the best location of the windows. Cut out the window material in the shape desired and baste it in place with #465 transfer tape and pins. Secure the outer edge of the window material to the inner side of the cover fabric. Then sew all around the outside of the window with a straight stitch. Next, cut out the window opening in the dodger fabric with a scissors. Allow an extra inch of fabric which can be folded under between the dodger and the window to form a neat hem. Secure this hem with a second row of straight stitches. You may want to use a separate strip of fabric hemmed to a finished width of about two inches to dress up the inner side of the window and to cover the raw edge of the plastic. This improves the appearance of the dodger from the inside, but it is not otherwise necessary (see Figure 10).

In warm climates it is often a good idea to provide the option of opening up the forward wall of the dodger. This can be done by placing a #10 zipper on each side of the front window. These can then be unzipped and the cover material rolled up and neatly tied.

To install the zippers, cut the fabric—allow at least 2 inches of material between your cut and the window edge. Then make up four strips of fabric two inches longer than your cuts and three inches wide. Hem the short ends of these strips and one long edge by folding under ½-inch and sewing it in place. Sew one side of a zipper cut to the same length as your fabric to the outer surface of the unhemmed side as shown in Figure 15. Make the end of the zipper flush with one end of the strip. Note that the #10 YKK zipper can be sewn in place running either direction. Then sew the second zipper half in place so that it mates properly with the first. Repeat these steps with the second set of strips and zipper halves.

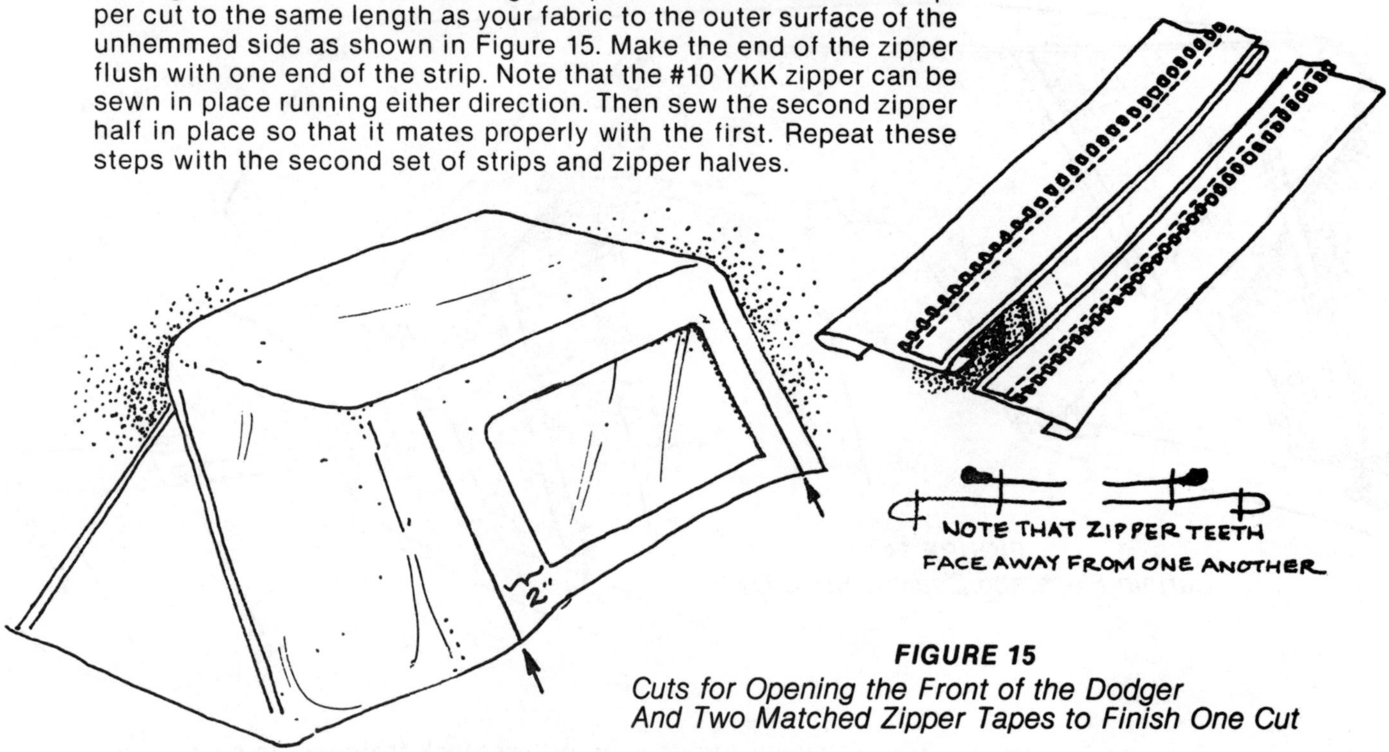

NOTE THAT ZIPPER TEETH
FACE AWAY FROM ONE ANOTHER

FIGURE 15
*Cuts for Opening the Front of the Dodger
And Two Matched Zipper Tapes to Finish One Cut*

Next sew the zipper strip assemblies onto the face of the dodger along your cuts. The edges of the cut fabric should be ½-inch inside the unfinished edges of the zipper tape and strip assemblies. Place a row of straight stitches along both long sides of the strip assemblies. The stitches on the zipper side should be near the teeth so they will catch the cut edge of the cover. Note that the two strip assemblies will overlap ½-inch.

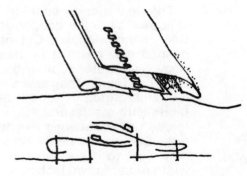

FIGURE 16
Sewing the Zipper Tapes in Place

Now fold the zipper edges under so they mate properly. It will be necessary to slit the zipper tape at the inner end of the cut in the fabric where the zipper teeth end. Run a row of straight stitches along the back of the teeth to hold them in place. A fold of the strip of cloth should partially cover the zipper teeth—this helps keep out water and it improves the appearance of your zipper installation (see Figure 14).

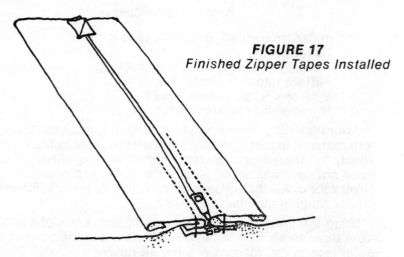

FIGURE 17
Finished Zipper Tapes Installed

Use a truncated triangle of leather roughly two inches on a side to reinforce the inside end of the zipper tape. Sew it on all three sides over the overlapping zipper tapes (see Figure 14). Also cover the last ¼-inch or so of the meshed zipper teeth with this leather. Sew round the teeth a couple of times with a hand needle and twine to lock them together.

Use a length of twine to whip the opposite ends of the zipper and to prevent the slider from coming off. Or you may prefer to sew a small leather tab in place here.

Sew six-inch strips of webbing or Velcro hook and loop tapes to opposite sides of the dodger just under the front bow and use these to hold the roll of material in place.

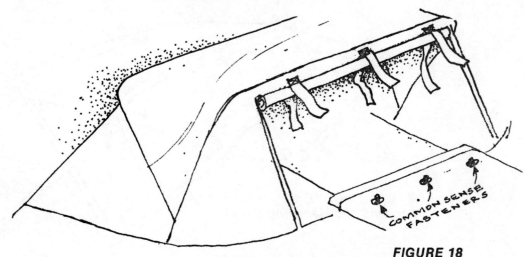

FIGURE 18
Straps for securing Rolled Dodger Section

The dodger is now complete. But leather or binding tape can be used anywhere there is an unfinished edge or an edge that may be subjected to unusual chafe. The use of these protective materials will add a note of quality to any dodger. Don't hesitate to use them freely.

Bimini Fabric Covers

The materials needed for Bimini tops include:
> Cover Cloth
> Roughly 16 feet of one-inch webbing
> Pattern paper or cloth
> V-69 or V-92 polyester thread
> Number 465 transfer tape

After installing the frame and taping it in position, tape your pattern material in place. It may well be necessary to tape two or more sheets of the pattern material together—go ahead. The pattern need not be made up of panels the same width as the expensive cover fabric. All that is necessary at this point is to determine the proper rough shape for the cover.

Bring the pattern round the curves along the sides of the frame from three to six inches down each side. Cut the pattern along the outer face of the forward and the aft bows.

Then use the pattern to cut the cover fabric. If more than one panel will be required, it is best to run the connecting seams in a fore and aft direction. This maintains the integrity of the unsupported edges of the cover. (But you may run the seams the other way if there is a significant savings in the yardage of cloth required.) Cut the panels to the length of your pattern with a ¾-inch seam allowance on both ends. Allow for at least a two-inch hem along both sides. Be careful to space the fore and aft seams evenly across the cover. If you will have an odd number of panels, start by cutting the one in the center. If there will be an even number, start with the two center ones. Allow a ½-inch seam allowance along each side of every panel required to make up the cover.

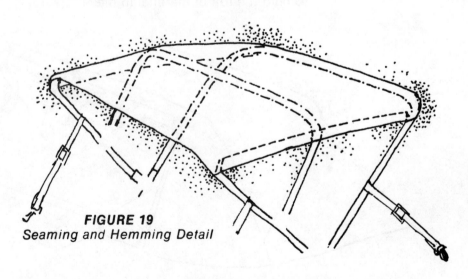

FIGURE 19
Seaming and Hemming Detail

Use this seam allowance to form semi-flat felled seams joining all the fore and aft panels. Fashion the two inch side hems by folding the fabric under and placing a row of straight stitches right along the folded edge. Keep the flap of the material underneath as you sew. This helps hold the fabric in place for the second row of stitches along the inner edge. It is a good idea to fold this inner edge under about ¼-inch to provide a proper finished appearance. Then place the assembly over your frame to be sure that it fits properly.

Now fashion sleeves at the front and the back of the cover for those bows. The sleeves are made by cutting four inch strips to match the curve of the edge in question. If you are using material with an obvious top and bottom (like vinyl coated Dacron), be sure to cut these strips "bottom side up."

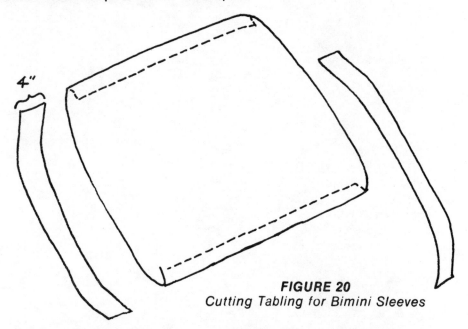

4"

FIGURE 20
Cutting Tabling for Bimini Sleeves

FIGURE 21
Detail of Bimini Sleeve Construction

Hem the ends of these strips by folding them up and over about ½-inch. Then place the strips bottom side up along the top of the appropriate edge. Run a row of straight stitches ½-inch inside the two matched edges. Then fold the strip out and hem its remaining long edge by folding under ¼-inch of fabric and holding it in place with a single row of straight stitches. (Again, it is best to sew this hem with the flap of fabric down as it goes through the machine.)

Then fold the strip all the way under the edge of the cover so that the seam joining the strip to the cover is at the leading (or trailing) edge of the fabric assembly. Use the transfer tape or staples or pins to hold the strip in place and run a row of straight stitches along the inside edge of the sleeve strip.

If there is a need for sleeves through the center of the cover for a third or fourth bow, make them up from cover cloth cut into 4 inch strips. Hem the strips all round—fold under ¼ inch of material. Then carefully pin or tape the strips in place and sew along both long edges. Center sleeves do not have to be full width. Their only purpose is to hold the bows in place. Indeed, it is possible to use snap tabs or even webbing ties instead of these sleeves through the center of the cover.

There are a number of options that can be used to finish the cover. For example, leather can be sewn to the outer side of the fore and aft sleeves. This looks good and it also protects this critical surface from chafe.

It is also possible to install snap fasteners or Velcro strips along both sides of the Bimini cover so that curtain panels can be attached to provide further protection from the sun. These panels will need to be tied down to the deck so they do not flap about in the wind.

9

Flags and Pennants

FLAGS AND PENNANTS

Flags are usually made of nylon, because it is relatively strong and it accepts bright dyes well. I prefer four-ounce oxford material for flags, but I have seen quite serviceable ones made of material as light as 3/4-ounce.

To make a set of signal flags, you will need red, white, blue, black, and yellow material. Also required will be V-46 thread, #465 transfer tape, webbing, and spur grommets.

There are no set rules for the size of signal flags, but a good rule of thumb is to make them 24 inches long and 18 inches high.

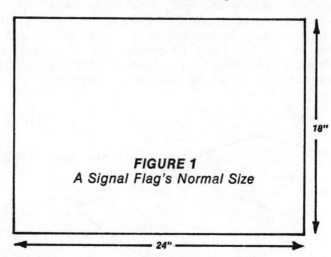

FIGURE 1
A Signal Flag's Normal Size

— Tack Line (roughly six inches long)

Fly

Hoist

There are two ways to build flags. If the design is complicated, it is best to applique it over the basic color or colors. For really intricate flags I recommend using nylon or Dacron adhesive backed insignia material on both sides of a four-ounce nylon base. The adhesive will hold even very thick portions of the design in place until they can be sewn with a zigzag stitch. The adhesive does, however, sometimes cause sewing problems — the machine may skip stitches when the needle becomes fouled. The use of a liquid silicone lubricant soaked cloth that is clipped over the top thread of the machine will help if this becomes a problem. But needles may still have to be changed rather frequently.

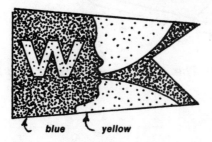

blue   yellow

FIGURE 2
The pennant for my own yacht club, Windjammers of Marina del Rey, California, can easily be made by appliqueing the blue design over a yellow background.

For moderately intricate designs four-ounce material can be basted to both sides of a four-ounce base with transfer tape. Sew the assembly together after it is complete with a zigzag stitch over all exposed edges.

While on the subject of edges, the insignia material introduced in the paragraph above can only be properly cut with scissors. But all other cutting of edges that will not be hemmed should be done with a hotknife (a soldering iron, soldering gun, or a wood burning tool will work nicely).

Simple designs such as those characteristic of the international signal flags should be made up of separate pieces of fabric of appropriate colors. It is best to join all the separate pieces with a flat felled seam, but quite serviceable flags are possible with simple overlapping seams (providing, of course, that all edges are heat-sealed). The use of transfer tape to baste all seams prior to sewing is a good idea unless you have extensive experience.

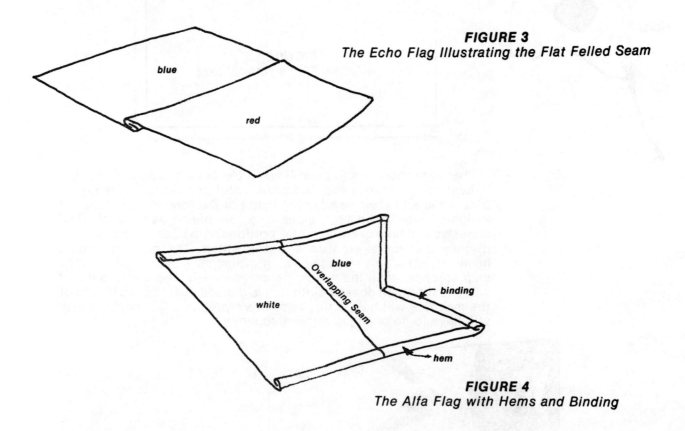

FIGURE 3
The Echo Flag Illustrating the Flat Felled Seam

FIGURE 4
The Alfa Flag with Hems and Binding

All outside edges of a flag (except the hoist side) should either be folded over 1/4 inch, folded again another 1/4 inch, and then sewn with a double row of stitches, or protected with an Orlon binding tape (generally available only in white). Place the first row of stitches right along the outside edge of the flag and the second over the inside edge of the hem or binding.

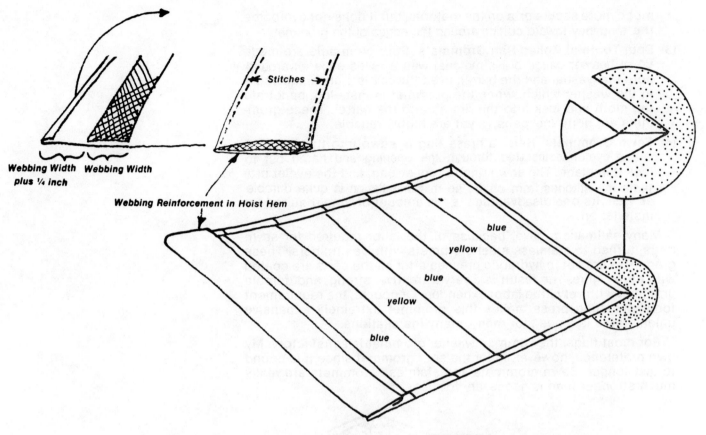

Webbing Width
plus ¼ inch

Webbing Width

Stitches

Webbing Reinforcement in Hoist Hem

blue
yellow
blue
yellow
blue

FIGURE 5
The Golf Flag with Fly Corner and Hoist Edge Details

The hoist side of the flag should be reinforced with a single thickness of webbing from 3/4 inch to two inches wide. Since the webbing is generally available only in white or black, it is a good idea to bury it in a wide hem as shown in Figure 5. Fold over 1/4 inch of the material and sew it in place with a row of straight stitches. Sew the webbing in place with straight stitches also. Keep the webbing parallel to the folded edge but back away from it the width of the webbing plus 1/4 inch or so. Fold this allowance over the webbing and sew it down with two rows of straight stitches—one just inside the folded edge and one along the other edge.

Grommets should be placed through the webbing on the hoist side of the flag. There are four kinds of grommets which can be used:

(1) **Common Washer Grommets.** The common washer grommet is very inexpensive but not very reliable. It is made up by simply sliding a thick brass washer over a brass barrel and flaring the latter with a special tool. The primary weakness with this grommet is its tendency to cut the cloth around it with its thin and rather sharp edges. It also is secured to the cloth by the clamping action only and can thus be pulled out with relatively little force.

(2) **Toothed Grommets.** The toothed grommet has small teeth all around the washer which lock into the cloth. That provides for a

much more secure grip on the material, but it does not overcome the tendency toward cutting around the edges of the grommet.

(3) **Spur-Toothed Rolled-Rim Grommets.** Spur grommets are made up of heavier gauge brass material with a rolled edge all around both the washer and the barrel. In addition, there are small spurs in the washer which, when the grommet is installed, penetrate the cloth and lock into the rim around the barrel. These grommets are quite inexpensive yet are highly reliable.

(4) **Sewn Grommets.** Here, a brass ring is sewn into the fabric. A brass eyelet is inserted through the opening and flared out to lock it in place. The sewn ring is very strong, and the eyelet protects the stitches from chafe, so this installation is quite durable as well. Its one disadvantage is the amount of time required for installation.

Many sailmakers have, because of the labor required for sewn rings, turned to stainless steel grommets with Delrin liners. These grommets are set in hydraulic presses after all the parts are coated with epoxy glue. The result is a very attractive, strong, and durable grommet with very little labor expended. Of course, the requirement for a hydraulic press makes this grommet extremely expensive unless there is a need for many, many installations.

For most flags, the common washer grommet is satisfactory. My own preference, however, is for the spur grommet since it is bound to last longer. Sewn grommets and stainless grommets are really much stronger than is necessary for flags.

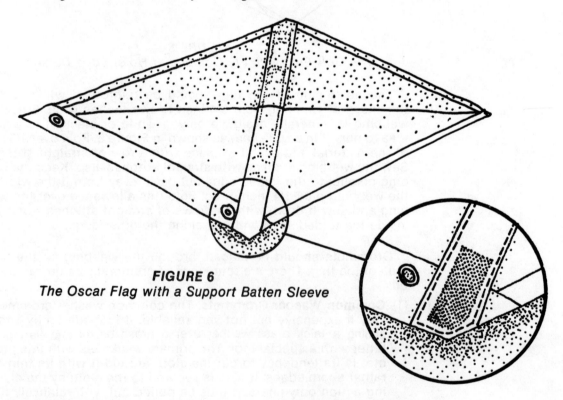

FIGURE 6
The Oscar Flag with a Support Batten Sleeve

In some cases, it will be desirable to build a support into the flag to keep it extended even when there is no wind. This is the case, for example, when making a man overboard pole flag (the "O" or Oscar flag). Such a support is not at all difficult to build into the flag. Simply sew a narrow band of cloth (hemmed or sealed on all edges) across the diagonal of the flag from the bottom of the hoist to the top of the fly along one side This band should be used to form a sleeve into which a narrow wood or plastic batten can be inserted. The band of cloth may, of course, have to be sewn of several colors, but this should cause no trouble. Be careful to reinforce the ends of the sleeve with leather or webbing to reduce the likelihood of chafe damage there.

The following plans are for a complete set of international flags. Note that most will be assembled of single thickness material. There are, however, a few with appliqued colors. Dimensions are all indicated below. Note that the grain of the cloth always runs perpendicular or horizontal to the hoist. This will avoid minor stress wrinkles in the flags. The size of the alphabet flags below will be 20 by 20 inches prior to hemming. This size was chosen to reduce yardage requirements. If your fabric is wider than 40 inches, you can easily increase the length of the flags to half of that width and still use the patterns below.

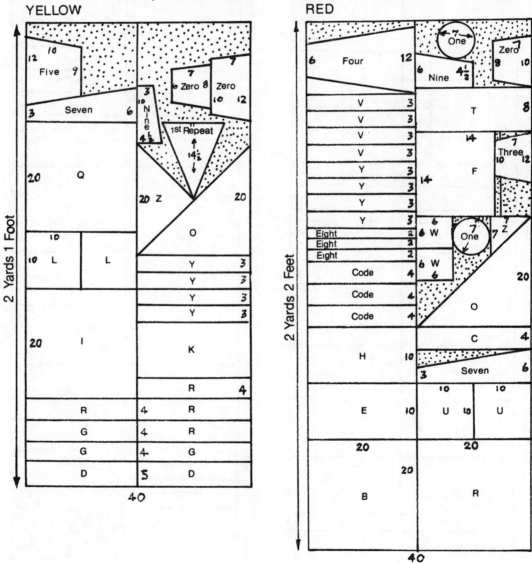

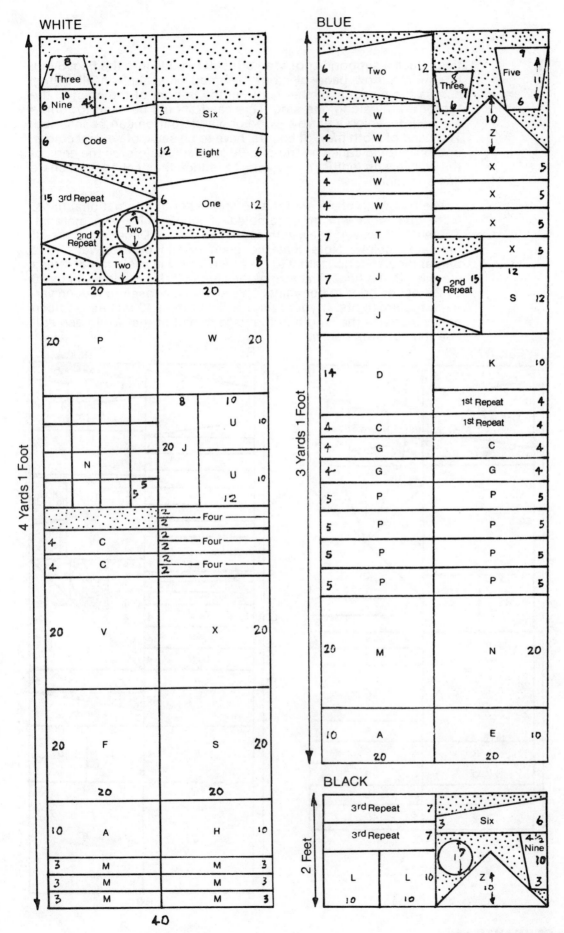

WHITE

BLUE

BLACK

INTERNATIONAL FLAGS AND PENNANTS

Alphabetical Flags			Numeral Pennants

Alphabetical Flags

Alfa — W B — Diver Down; Keep Clear

Bravo — R — Dangerous Cargo

Charlie — B R B R B — Yes

Delta — Y B Y — Keep Clear

Echo — B R — Altering Course to Starboard

Foxtrot — W R — Disabled

Golf — Y B — Want a Pilot

Hotel — W R — Pilot on Board

India — Y Bl — Altering Course to Port

Juliett — B W B — On Fire; Keep Clear

Kilo — Y B — Desire to Communicate

Lima — Y Bl Bl Y — Stop Instantly

Mike — B W — I Am Stopped

November — B W — No

Oscar — R Y — Man Overboard

Papa — B W — About to Sail

Quebec — Y — Request Pratique

Romeo — R Y — Engines Going Astern

Sierra — W B — Engines Going Astern

Tango — R W B — Keep Clear of Me

Uniform — R W W R — Standing into Danger

Victor — R W — Require Assistance

Whiskey — B R — Require Medical Assistance

Xray — W B — Stop Your Intention

Yankee — Y R — Am Dragging Anchor

Zulu — Y Bl B R — Require a Tug

REPEATERS

1st Repeat — Y B

2nd Repeat — B W

3rd Repeat — W Bl

R CODE — W — Code and Answering Pennant (Decimal Point)

Numeral Pennants

1 — R W

2 — W B

3 — R W B

4 — R W

5 — Y B

6 — Bl W

7 — Y R

8 — R W

9 — W Bl R Y

0 — Y R Y

B = Blue   R = Red   W = White   Y = Yellow   Bl = Black

10

Harnesses

TRAPEZE AND SAFETY HARNESSES

Harnesses can be made up for any number of purposes to fit many different sizes of people. But the principles of construction are universal. I will simply present one trapeze harness and two safety harness designs here. Feel free to modify them as you like to fit your special requirements.

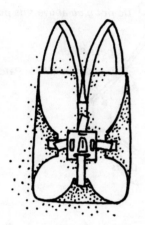

Trapeze Harnesses

Trapeze harnesses are used by some one-design classes to provide much more effective use of crew weight (and sometimes the helmsman's weight too) as ballast. If nothing else, they make sailing more exciting and physically demanding.

Begin your work by assembling all of the materials that you will need. The following is a representative list:

> Four-ounce nylon oxford cloth
> V-46 polyester thread
> Buckle with trapeze hook (I prefer that made by Holt Allen and have assumed it in what follows)
> 8 feet of webbing (1½ inches wide) — a wider 2-inch webbing is sometimes more appropriate for the crotch strap depending on the buckle used
> Adhesive (#465 tape or silicone seal)
> Ensolite flotation material (25'' x 18'')
> Velcro tape (5/8'' x 9'')

Use a piece of inexpensive cloth or paper to fashion a pattern for your trapeze. The pattern should look somewhat like the shape shown in Figure 1. Cut and trim until you achieve the shape that offers you greatest comfort.

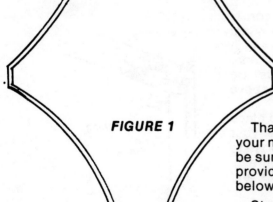

FIGURE 1

That pattern should then be used to cut two harness panels from your nylon cloth. Use a pen or pencil to trace around the pattern. But be sure to cut the panels out roughly 3/4 inch outside your outline to provide a seam allowance. Also trace the patches indicated below—these, too, should be cut a bit larger than your pattern.

Study these instructions until you understand them. Then proceed with the work in the order indicated.

1. Glue or tape the two cloth harness panels together with pattern lines out. Be careful to secure only the outside half inch or so of the fabric panels to permit turning the assembly inside out later. Do not glue above the point indicated in Figure 2 below.

2. Glue or tape the 7 corner patches to one side of the assembly. Note that there are two patches in the crotch of the harness and one across the shoulders and 2 along the sides. The large chest and crotch patches go on first. The smaller chest and crotch patches overlap them.

3. Start sewing just below the shoulder side of the assembly (at one arrow Figure 2) and sew down and around it with a row of straight stitches ¾-inch inside the edge. Stop sewing just below the shoulder side of the assembly opposite where you began (at the other arrow in Figure 2).

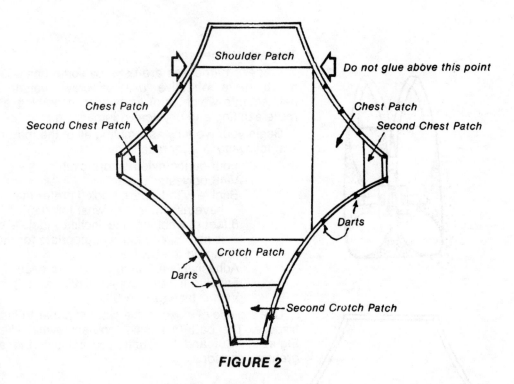

FIGURE 2

4. Cut darts of cloth out of the seam allowance at each corner and clip small darts along the inside curves of the seam allowance along the sides. (see Figure 2). That will make it possible to turn everything inside out through the shoulder opening without bunching the seam allowance inside. Be careful not to cut into your seams and do not clip darts above the arrows.

5. With the fabric assembly now right side out, you should place another row of straight stitches all round the harness over your first stitching installed above. Keep these stitches as close to the edge of the assembly as possible (stitch "1" in Figure 3). The only purpose of this stitching is to finish the edges and flatten them.

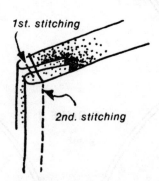

6. Sew across the inside ends of the smaller chest and crotch patches as illustrated in Figure 3 (stitch "2").

7. Cut two flotation blocks to fit and insert them in the harness sides as indicated in Figure 4.

8. Place a row of stitches along the inside of the flotation blocks to lock them in place (stitch "3" in Figure 3).

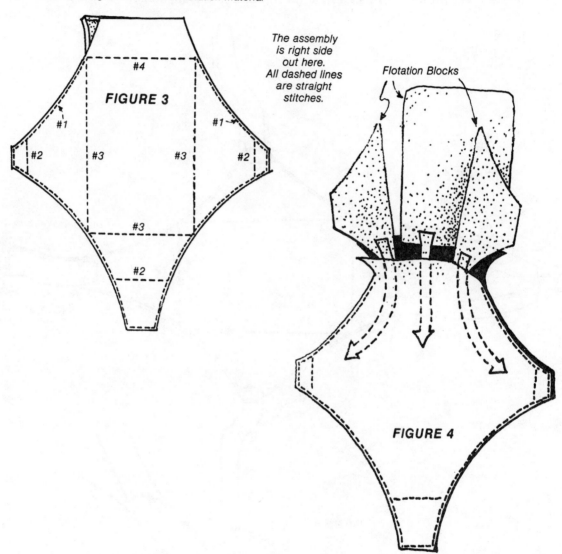

Unsewn opening for insertion of flotation material

FIGURE 3

The assembly is right side out here. All dashed lines are straight stitches.

Flotation Blocks

FIGURE 4

9. Insert the large central block of flotation material after first cutting it to shape (see grayed area Figure 4).

10. Sew across the top of the central flotation block to lock it in place (stitch "4" in Figure 3). Another row of stitches just above the first may be necessary to secure the inner edge of the top patch.

11. Tuck under the flaps of cloth at the top of harness and place a row of stitches all around the top as close to the edge as possible. A little glue or tape will help hold the flaps and the panels in place.

12. Cut webbing to the lengths indicated in Figure 5. Add an extra two inches to each length to provide an overlap for sewing them to the harness. Seal the ends with a soldering gun or wood burning tool to prevent raveling. Sew all but the bottom strap (the one that holds on the buckle) to the harness as indicated. Try on the harness and align the straps if necessary.

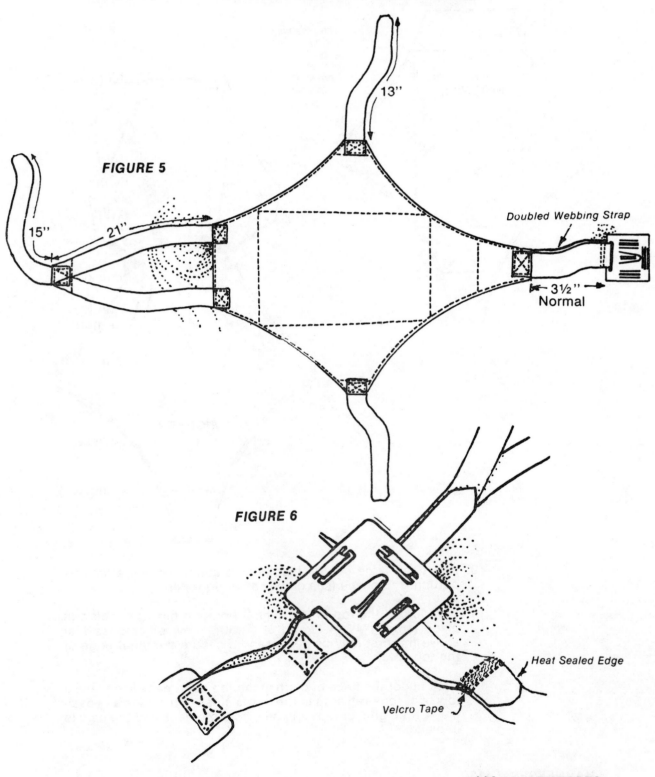

FIGURE 5

13"

15"

21"

Doubled Webbing Strap

3½"
Normal

FIGURE 6

Heat Sealed Edge

Velcro Tape

13. Now sew the buckle to the harness with a double length of webbing as illustrated in Figure 6.

14. Put on the harness and tighten the straps. Secure Velcro tabs to the strap ends to keep them in place. They should lie flat against the harness when the straps are comfortably tight. See Figure 6.

SAFETY HARNESSES

I have seen some very complex safety harnesses which are probably extremely useful in some circumstances where the utmost in security is required. Unfortunately those harnesses are generally so difficult to put on and so uncomfortable to wear that they are seldom used except in the most extreme circumstances.

The two safety harnesses described here are extremely simple and remarkably comfortable, yet they are also perfectly adequate for any life saving emergency likely to be experienced by life-long cruising sailors. Even so, I am presenting two harness designs below to provide a measure of choice. The "regular" safety harness is of standard design with a single safety hook. The second design is an ingenious invention by Joy Laughenburger intended to provide three additional benefits:

1. Instant adjustability over a broad range of sizes to accommodate crew and clothing changes.

2. A "sling" effect which makes getting hoisted back on board much more comfortable than it otherwise is—a normal harness tends to strangle its wearer.

3. Two safety hooks which permit leapfrogging from point to point on the boat without ever being detached.

Joy has cruised many miles with the "Laughenburger Harness," and her experience along with that of many Sailrite Kit customers leads me to recommend it very highly.

Now, let's get to the actual construction of the two harnesses.

Regular Safety Harness

The following is a representative list of the materials needed to build a regular safety harness:

FIGURE 7

THE REGULAR SAFETY HARNESS

10 Feet of 1½-inch webbing
Two #1 D-rings
13 Feet of one-inch safety webbing
One safety hook
V-69 Polyester thread
Buckle for adjustment (optional)
Velcro tape to secure excess webbing (needed only with the adjustable harness)

Study the above drawing (Figure 7) carefully. Note that the shoulder straps are free to slide on the chest belt. The shoulder straps should cross over in the back.

The construction process takes place in five stages:

1. Cut two 30-inch strips of webbing with a soldering gun or other hot instrument so that it will not ravel. Fold over three inches at each end of both strips and sew the resulting loops down with a one-inch "Box-X" stitch to form a two-inch-long opening. These two lengths of webbing are the shoulder straps (Figure 8).

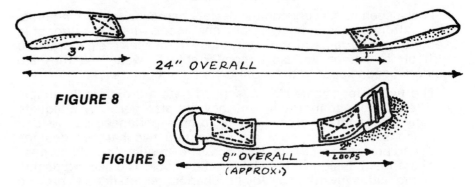

3" 24" OVERALL 1"

FIGURE 8

8" OVERALL
(APPROX.) 2" LOOPS

FIGURE 9

2. Cut a nine-inch strip of webbing with the soldering gun. Insert one end through a D-ring and one end through the buckle, as shown above. Fold two inches of webbing over both pieces of hardware and sew these loops down as before with a "Box-X" stitch. See Figure 9. This length is the short chest belt.

3. Insert one end of the remaining webbing through the second D-ring and fold back two inches. Sew it fast with the "Box-X" stitch. Now roll the other end into a tight tube to three thicknesses. Sew this down with a row of straight stitches (Figure 10). This "bump" will prevent the harness coming completely apart if the buckle slips.

FIGURE 10

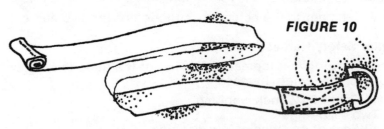

FIGURE 11

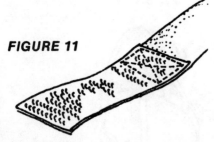

4. With the 1½-inch strips of Velcro, fashion a small "backstrap" which will be used to hold the two D-rings together during normal boating activity (under strain the nylon safety line takes over this function). Sew the tapes end-to-end with a half-inch overlap so that the hook faces up and the loop faces down.

5. Make a three-inch loop in one end of the safety webbing. Sew it carefully with a Box-X stitch that is one-inch long. Secure the safety hook to the other end with a second, shorter loop.

6. Now assemble the harness and check it for fit. Make any adjustments necessary. Note that the safety hook goes through

the D-rings and then through the webbing loop. Pull it all the way through to hold the D-rings together.

The Laughenburger Safety Harness

The representative list of materials follows:

12 Feet of two-inch safety webbing
Two #2 D-rings
Four inches of Velcro tape
13 Feet of one-inch safety webbing
Two safety hooks
V-69 Polyester thread
One 1¾-inch stainless ring

Study the above drawing carefully. Note that the shoulder straps are centered on the back of the chest belt and that they are free to slide on the forward side. This is the key to the support and the adjustability of the Laughenburger harness. It can be worn by people large and small with bulky clothing or not—yet, when tension is applied to the safety line, the harness tightens securely.

The construction process take place in seven stages:

1. Cut two 39-inch strips of webbing with a soldering gun or other hot instrument so that it will not ravel. Fold over three inches at the end of both strips and sew the resulting loops down with a one-inch "Box-X" stitch to form a two-inch-long opening. These two lengths of webbing are the shoulder straps. See Figure 12.

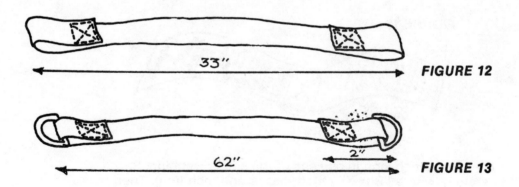

33"

FIGURE 12

62"   2"

FIGURE 13

2. Insert each end of the remaining webbing through the two D-rings. Fold two inches of webbing over both pieces of hardware and sew these loops down as before with a "Box-X" stitch. This length is the chest belt. See Figure 13.

3. Thread the chest belt through the loops in the shoulder straps so that the harness looks like the finished drawing. Stitch the back shoulder loops to the belt approximately three inches apart on the center of the chest belt. Also stitch the straps together where they cross on the wearer's back.

4. Sew a four-inch piece of one-inch webbing to one front shoulder loop after first looping it through the stainless ring

and folding it over one inch. Use a "Box-X" stitch to secure it in both places. (See Figure 14, right side, for a detail of this installation.)

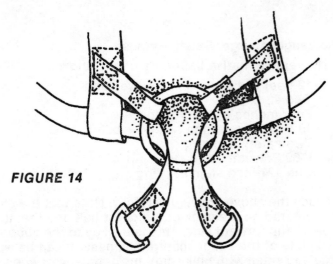

FIGURE 14

5. With the two-inch strip of Velcro, fashion a small strap which will be used to hold the harness in place during normal boating activity (under strain, the nylon safety line and the chest belt take over this function). Sew the parts together end-to-end with a half-inch overlap so that both faces are up (Figure 15). Sew this strap to the forward loop of the shoulder strap that does not have the stainless steel ring so that it can be looped around the stainless ring and tacked together on itself (Figure 14 left side).

FIGURE 15

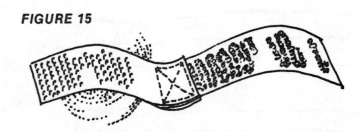

6. Make a three-inch loop in one end of the safety webbing. Sew it carefully with a "Box-X" stitch that is one inch long. Then slide a safety hook onto the other end of the webbing. Form a loop in the webbing at roughly the center of its length and use a "Box-X" stitch to close it around this first hook there. Secure the second safety hook to the other unfinished end of the webbing with a second, shorter loop.

The harness will fit just about anyone in its present form, but, if it will normally be worn by one person, it will be more comfortable if the shoulder straps are shortened until the chest belt is roughly three inches or so under the armpits. Also shorten the chest belt until its two ends hang no more than three inches out of the breast ring. To shorten the straps, simply double them back on themselves and sew the three layers in place with another "Box-X" stitch. This makes it possible to increase the size of the harness later on.

11

Sail and Ditty Bags

SAIL AND DITTY BAGS

Sail and ditty bags are meant to offer inexpensive protection from chafe and dirt. Four-ounce oxford-finished nylon fabric best meets these needs — its availability in a wide variety of colors is an extra bonus. Sail bags are usually not made of a waterproofed nylon though there are some who prefer it. If you do use the waterproofed material, be sure to warn all who might use the bags to dry sails thoroughly before storing them. If the waterproofed material prevents the entrance of moisture, it also must prevent its exit.

Other fabrics ranging from acrylics and Dacron cover cloth to Dacron sailcloth—even spinnaker cloth—can be used, depending upon your special requirements.

The most common thread for bags of all kinds is V-46 polyester, but you may use heavier or lighter thread without problems, if you like.

There are three basic bag designs:

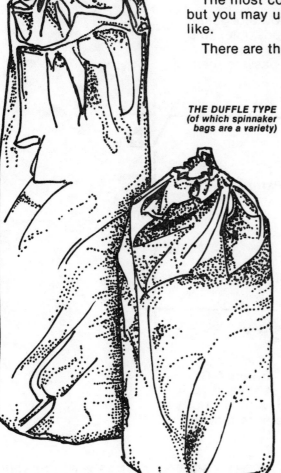

THE DUFFLE TYPE
(of which spinnaker bags are a variety)

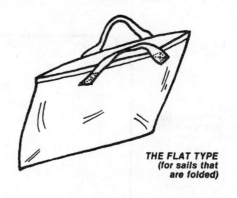

THE FLAT TYPE
(for sails that are folded)

THE FOREDECK TYPE
(in which sails are stored hanked on the forestay)

Let's consider each in turn.

DUFFLE BAGS

Duffle bags are usually made in one of two ways. Small ones can be fashioned quickly and easily of a single piece of cloth. Larger bags will require a separate piece of fabric for the bottom and the barrel.

Smaller Bags.

The size of the bag possible with the first technique will depend upon the size of the fabric piece used. This bag will have a square bottom and each side of the square will equal roughly ¼ of the base length of the fabric. The bag's height will be the height of the fabric less two inches (for seams and the top hem) and less ¼ of the fabric's base (to allow for the bottom fold). To fashion this bag, follow the step-by-step instructions below.

1. Cut the material to proper size with the figure below as a guide. Use a soldering iron or gun to do the cutting if possible. This "hotknife" will seal the cloth at the same time that it is cut. If a hotknife is not available, sear the raw edges by passing them briefly over a candle flame.

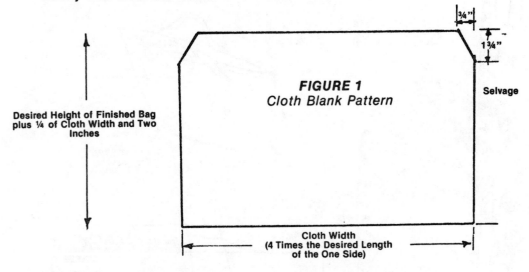

FIGURE 1
Cloth Blank Pattern

¾"

1 ¾"

Selvage

Desired Height of Finished Bag
plus ¼ of Cloth Width and Two
Inches

Cloth Width
(4 Times the Desired Length
of the One Side)

2. Roll over 1/4-inch of fabric at the two cutoff corners.* Sew these two short hems in place with one row of straight stitches. Each sewn seam should begin and end with a short "backstitch" or reversal of the machine to be sure that the stitch does not come undone.

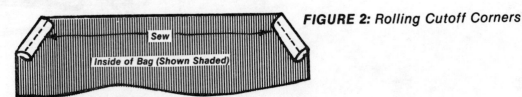

FIGURE 2: *Rolling Cutoff Corners*

Sew

Inside of Bag (Shown Shaded)

*Note that a second method of providing for the drawstring exit is described in the larger duffle bag instructions. That method (utilizing a grommet) can be employed instead of this one if you prefer.

3. Form a 1¼-inch hem along the top of the material (the side bordered by the two short corner hems just fashioned). Do this by first folding over 1/4-inch of material and then 1¼-inch more so that the inside edge will be protected. Place two rows of straight stitches along the doubled portion of the hem. It is a good idea to use pins or staples to baste the hem in place before you sew.

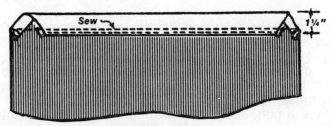

FIGURE 3: *Top Hem*

4. Now fold the material in half vertically so that the hem just fashioned is on the outside. Sew the open side shut using a straight seam 1/2 inch inside the edges. Then roll the 1/2 inch seam allowance to 1/4 inch and run a row of straight stitches over the roll, securing the seam allowance flat to the wall of the bag.

5. Run a row of straight stitches across the bottom of the folded material. Place these stitches roughly 1/4-inch from the two matched bottom edges of the cloth.

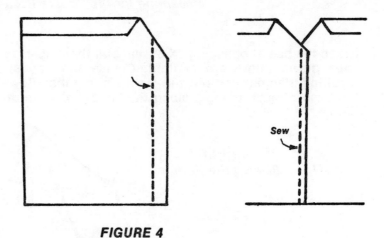

FIGURE 4
Side Seam Detail

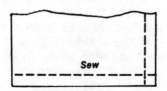

FIGURE 5: Bottom Seam

6. Now make the flat bottom for the bag. Measure the width of the bag from center fold to the stitch line opposite it. Divide the measured width by 4. Mark "X's" at the two points on the bag one-quarter of the width up from the bottom of the bag and in from the sides (in both cases, measure from seam lines if they are present). Use a pin to pierce the bag at each "X" and mark where it penetrates on the opposite side with another set of "X's"—from each of the four "X's" draw lines straight down to the bottom of the bag.

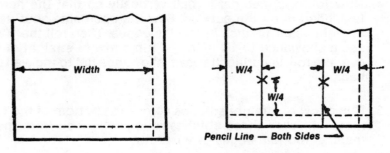

FIGURE 6
Measuring for the Square Bottom

7. Grasp the bag at opposing "X's" and pull them apart until the lines drawn above are straight. Crease the edges of the resulting triangles of cloth and pin them together. Sew across the base of each triangle along the lines that were drawn in Step 6.

FIGURE 7
Sewing the Bottom

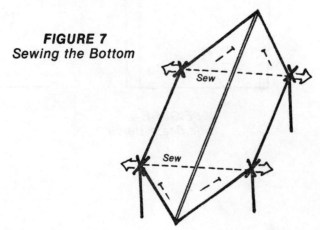

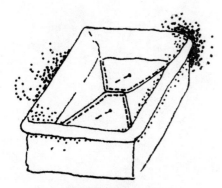

FIGURE 8
*Using the Triangular Flaps
as Bottom Reinforcement*

8. The triangles of extra cloth can either be cut away now and the resulting raw edge rolled and sewn or they can be used to reinforce the bottom of the bag. If you choose to do the latter, turn the bag right side out and roll down the sides. Pin the triangular flaps of cloth in place against the bottom of the bag. Then run straight stitches along their edges starting in the center of the bottom and moving to the corners.

9. With the bag right side out, use a safety pin to fish the drawstring through the top hem. When both parts of the drawstring exit the rolled hems at each end of the sleeve along the top of the bag, tie the ends together with a simple overhand knot.

10. The bag can be labeled if you like. Use an indelible laundry marking pen. Lay several thicknesses of newspaper inside the bag and place it flat on a suitable surface. Use masking tape as upper and lower guide lines for your lettering. Since sails are often stacked in forward vee berths, it is a good idea to label the bottom of each bag as well as its side (Figure 9).

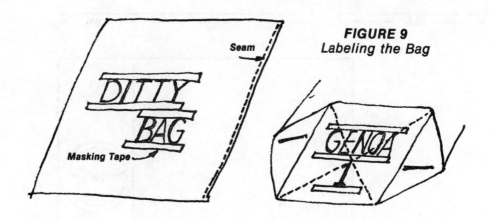

FIGURE 9
Labeling the Bag

Larger Duffle Bags

The second method of building duffle type bags entails the use of two pieces of material: one for the round bottom and one for the barrel of the bag. A bit of care is required to match the circular end piece to the barrel properly but, if these instructions are carefully followed, there should be no serious trouble.

I. The first step of construction is to indicate cutting and sewing lines on the cloth.

A. Use a short length of string to form the circular piece for each bag. The basic circle will have a diameter equal to that of the finished bag. This is the line which will guide your sewing. A second circle with a diameter 1½ inches greater should be drawn around the first one. This indicates the cutting line for the end piece in question.

B. The barrel should be as long as the circumference of the inside ring of the bottom circle plus 1½ inches for a side seam allowance. The circumference of a circle is Pi times D where Pi equals 3.1416 and D equals the diameter of the circle.

C. Cut the barrel and the end piece from the cloth. Use a soldering gun or a wood burning tool to accomplish this if possible since the hot blade will fuse and seal the cloth at the same time it is cut. If this "hotknife" is not available, pass the raw edges of the cloth through a candle flame to sear them.

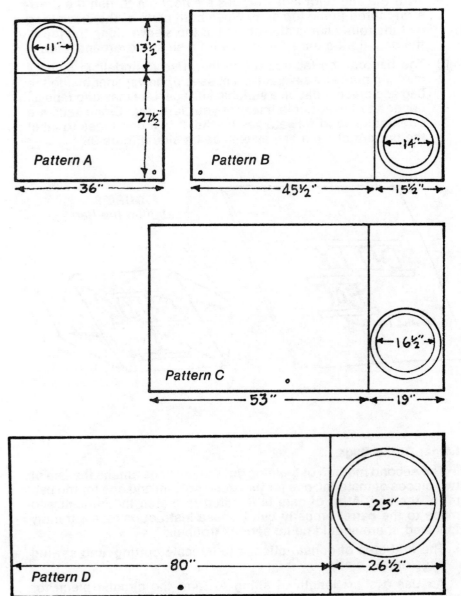

FIGURE 10
Representative Patterns for Larger Round Bottom Sail Bags

II. Now proceed to the actual sewing.

  A. First sew the end piece to the long edge (the one that will be "on the bottom" of the bag) of the barrel—the one without grommets.

    1. Place the end piece on the barrel cloth. Move the circle so that its diameter lies parallel to one short edge of the barrel cloth, but about two inches inside of it and tangent to one long edge.

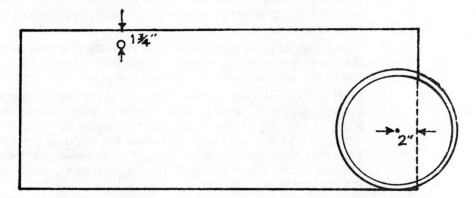

FIGURE 11
Sewing the Base onto the Barrel

    2. Using a straight (not zigzag) stitch, sew the end piece to the barrel down the line indicated along the edge of the circle. Keep the edge of the barrel piece even with the edge of the circle. This will mean that you will need to carefully rotate the circle as you sew. Its seam allowance will pucker as you do this. That is perfectly normal. I find it helpful to use pins to baste the circle to the barrel prior to sewing. Push the pins into the fabric at 90° to the seam—you will then be able to sew right over them. Sew to within two inches of the second short barrel edge.

    3. The barrel piece should reach all the way round the end piece with at least one-inch overlap. If there is more overlap, do not worry about it. If there is less, rip the seam just put in and sew the end piece to the barrel along a line from 1/8 to 1/4-inch inside your original end piece circular line. (A careful pinning job in step 2 above will avoid this time consuming process.)

  B. Now match the short edges of the barrel piece together (these edges will run vertically up the side of the finished bag). Inside these matched edges from ½ to 2½ inches (depending upon the seam allowance left after stitching the bottom in place), run a row of straight stitches. Sew from the top of the bag right through to the bottom where the end piece is attached. Then finish sewing all around the circumference of the end piece (two inches were left unsewn on both sides of the barrel seam in Step II/A/2). This should attach it securely to the barrel everywhere.

C. Install the drawstring in the top of the bag next. (Note that another method of installing the drawstring is described in the small duffle bag instructions — it can be used instead of this one if you prefer.)

1. Roll over 1/4 inch of the fabric along the top of the bag and to the outside. Sew it in place with a row of straight stitches. Insert a #1 Spur Grommet 1½ inches from the rolled edge. Then fold over the top edge of the barrel again to form a 1¼-inch hem. Note that this hem will be on the inside of the bag when it is turned right side out. Crease the fold down well.

2. Insert the piece of braided Dacron drawstring into a grommet and lay it along the crease in the hem. Make sure that the string will be inside the hem when it is sewn shut.

3. Start at the grommet and sew the hem to the barrel using a straight stitch. It helps to sew this hem with it under the edge of the bag as the fabric goes through the machine. You will find that it is easy to follow the edge of the hem under the bag even though it cannot be seen—it will be an obvious bump. Be sure to keep the drawstring well into the fold all along the way.

4. As you approach the point where you began sewing, run the free end of the drawstring through the original grommet or through a second one near the first if you prefer a separate grommet for each side of the drawstring. Finish the stitching along the hem. This will completely enclose the drawstring except where it exits at the grommet or grommets.

5. Cut the drawstring at whatever length you desire. Tie knots at the ends of the drawstring to keep it from disappearing through the grommet(s).

D. Turn the bag right side out. It is done!

FIGURE 12
Sewing a Hem with the Flap Underneath

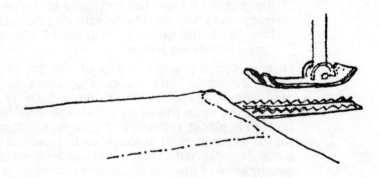

SPINNAKER LAUNCHING BAGS

Spinnaker bags are modifications of either the small or large duffle bags. They feature a hoop at their mouths which keeps them open. This makes it possible to carefully pack the sails and launch them directly from the bags which are intended to be hung from the forestay, the bow pulpit, or a shroud. With their shock cord secured lid, these bags will keep the spinnaker packed with just its head and clews showing until the halyard is raised. This automatically removes the lid and releases the chute without twists.

In addition to the four-ounce nylon fabric and V-46 thread required for regular duffle bags, you will need a bit of sail twine and a sailmaker's needle, ring material (I like to use Cycolac—also known as ABS—batten material in a 5/8-inch or one-inch width—two proprietary names are "Recmar" and "White Flo"), nylon shock cord (size is not critical but I generally use 3/16-inch cord), a couple of boat hook snaps or jib snaps, and some lengths of 3/4-inch or one-inch nylon webbing.

FIGURE 14
A Finished Spinnaker Launching Bag

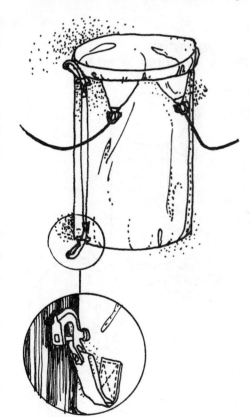

Begin your work by completing a duffle bag following either of the two procedures outlined previously, but do not sew the top hem or install the drawstring. The diameter of the bag should be rather large compared to a normal sail bag in order to make packing and launching easier. I suggest 12 inches as the minimum diameter. Sails between 300 and 700 square feet should have bags with 18-inch diameter openings and larger sails should have 24-inch diameter openings. Because of their large diameter, spinnaker bags are seldom more than 24 inches in height, but allow for a good deal more height than you think you will need since that dimension can be shortened as necessary to provide a perfect fit when the ring is installed.

After the lower part of the bag has been fashioned, make up the Cycolac ring and install it. The ring should equal the circumference of the bag in length plus 3¼ inches to allow for an overlap. Form the proper ring with just that overlap. Using a five-foot length of doubled sail twine, whip the overlapped portion just as you would a piece of rope:

1. Form a loop in the end of the twine.

2. Place the loop on the overlapped ends of the ring.

3. Now bind the two ends together by wrapping them with the twine.

4. Continue wrapping until you have covered the entire overlapped portion of the ring.

5. Run the end of the twine through the loop (which should still be exposed) and pull hard on the end of the twine so that the loop is tightened and the free end of the twine is drawn under the whipping.

FIGURE 15
Whipping the Rings Ends Together

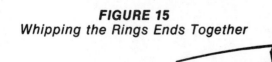

FIGURE 16
Measuring the Sail for Proper Bag Height

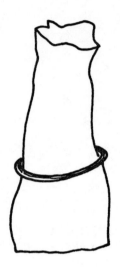

Now pack the spinnaker in the bag. Do not hesitate to pack it tightly since a smaller bag will be easier to handle on a wet, pitching deck. Slide the ring over the top of the bag and mark or crease the fabric well to indicate what will be the lip of the bag.

Turn the bag inside out. Cut the top of the bag off so that there will be a 2½-inch hem allowance beyond your creased line. Fold out and down a 1/2-inch roll of cloth along the top edge of the bag. Sew this hem in place if you find that it is difficult to hold it in place for the stitches that follow. Then fold out and down a 2¼-inch hem to form a sleeve or pocket for the ring.

Sew this hem in place on the outside of the bag (while it is inside out) with the ring inside that hem. I like to keep the flap of cloth underneath as it goes through the machine since that enables the feed dogs to exert pressure on both the flap and the body of the bag as well. Go slowly and be sure that you do not pucker the cloth. A few basting pins or stitches would be a good idea. Keep your stitches straight and accurate since they will be visible when the bag is done.

FIGURE 17
Attaching Snaps Along the Barrel Seam

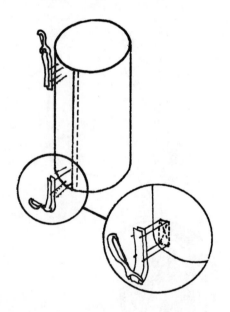

Now turn the bag right side out. Cut two eight-inch strips of webbing. Use these folded strips to secure boat snaps near the top and the bottom of the bag along the vertical seam. Sew the strips to the bag with several passes through the machine to be sure that they will not come off. I like to use the "Box-x" stitch for this (simply make a square of straight stitches and run acrcss the two diagonals of the box thus formed with two more lines of straight stitches).

The lid should be made up of two pieces of fabric. The first is a circle equal to the diameter of the bag's opening plus 3½ inches. The second is a ring of fabric with the same outside diameter but with a hole in its center one inch less than the diameter of the bag. The result in this second case, of course, is a ring of cloth 4½ inches wide.

Fasten the ring of cloth to the circle with a row of straight stitches within ¼-inch of their two matched outer edges. Then turn the assembly inside out through the opening in the ring so that the seam allowance is buried inside.

Roll under ¼-inch of the inside edge of the ring and stitch that rolled edge down to the lid circle all round except for a one- or two-inch opening into which you can insert the shock cord. Be sure to baste this seam carefully before sewing it.

Cut a length of shock cord equal to 93% of the circumference of the opening of the bag. Work it all round the pocket formed on the lid circle.

FIGURE 18
The Two-Piece Lid Construction

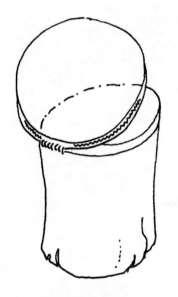

FIGURE 19
Detail of the Lid Attachment

Bring the two ends of the shock cord out of the opening in the pocket. Overlap them ¾-inch and sew them together carefully with a doubled length of sail twine. Penetrate both cords and wrap them several times; then penetrate them again at the opposite end of the wrapped portion. Finally, tuck the shock cord inside its pocket and sew the pocket shut.

Sew the lid to the barrel near the vertical seam with your needle and sail twine. Go through the barrel about one inch below the plastic ring, around the shock cord in the lid, and back through the barrel near your first penetration. Repeat this stitch from five to ten times. Sew under the loose ends of the twine and cut it off neatly.

FLAT BAGS

Flat bags are especially appropriate for racing skippers who like to fold their sails after each use. As you can imagine, this is generally possible only with smaller sails used on day sailing boats. But, whenever possible, it should be encouraged since the efficient life of the sails will be greatly prolonged.

Start with a piece of fabric twice as long as the desired height of the bag and the same width as that desired for the bag.

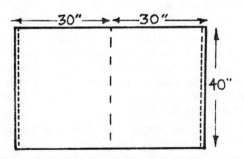

FIGURE 20
A Representative Flat Sail Bag Pattern

Finish the two ends across the width of the material by creasing over ¼-inch of material and then folding over a second time to a depth of one inch to form finished hems. Sew this double hem in place on each side of the bag with two rows of straight stitches. The first should be within 1/8-inch of the outside edge of the material.

Then fold the cloth along its center so that the hems are opposite one another and outside the bag (it will be sewn together inside out and then reversed). Use a straight stitch within ½-inch of the two ends of the bag to close them. Be sure to stitch the top corners very well as there will be a good deal of strain here.

Turn the bag right side out and secure roughly 12-inch long strips of webbing to the center of each top edge to form handles. The two base points for each handle should be about six inches apart. I like to use the "Box-x" stitch to secure the webbing.

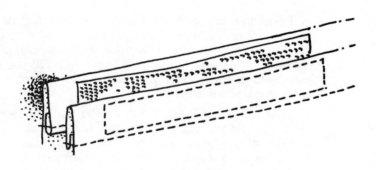

FIGURE 21
Details of the Top "Closure" Edges of a Flat Bag

Cut three-inch long pieces of Velcro hook and loop tape to form closures for the bag. Secure these with straight stitches all around them at roughly 12-inch intervals all along the open side of the bag.

FOREDECK BAGS

Foredeck bags make foresail storage very convenient and they relieve the inner space storage that plagues all boat owners. And, so long as the covers are well-made of durable polyester or acrylic cover material, the sails that they protect will not be harmed at all.

There are many possible foredeck bag patterns, but I like the ones below best. They are easy to make and very easy to use—the sail can be stowed or broken out in practically no time at all. The bags are essentially nothing more than a length of cloth which is placed under the sail, brought up around both sides of it and then secured along the front and back.

I. Cut the fabric according to the appropriate pattern from among those provided in Figure 23a.
    A. Cut away the wedges of cloth along the forward side of the bag material. Note that the center should be left flat to provide a tack opening. This flat section is off center so that a flap will be formed to close the bag along its leading edge.

Foredeck Bag Pattern and Yardage Requirements								
Bag Size	**F2**		**F3**		**F4**		**F5**	
Sails to be covered:								
Working sails to	100 sq. ft.		200 sq. ft.		300 sq. ft.		400 sq. ft.	
Medium air sails to	175 sq. ft.		275 sq. ft.		400 sq. ft.		500 sq. ft.	
Light air sails to	250 sq. ft.		350 sq. ft.		500 sq. ft.		600 sq. ft.	
Width of Fabric	36-42	30-35	36-42	30-35	36-42	30-35	36-42	30-35
Pattern required:	A	E	B	F	C	G	D	H
Cloth needed:	6 ft.	7 ft.	9 ft.	10'8"	12 ft.	16 ft.	14 ft.	19 ft.

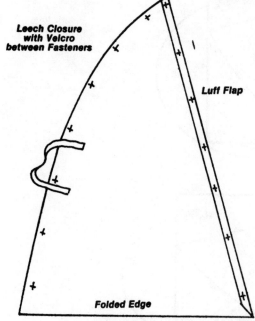

Leech Closure with Velcro between Fasteners

Luff Flap

Folded Edge

FIGURE 22
The Finished Foredeck Bag

B . If the pattern which you are using calls for the addition of two triangles of cloth to increase the cover's length, use the triangles cut away from the front edge in Step A above. Join the two triangles together along the short edges adjacent to the right angle. Lay one directly on top of the other and run a row of straight stitches one-half inch inside the two edges to be joined. Then fold the top triangle out. Lay this assembly directly over the top of the main cover panel so that its long straight edge is flush with the aft edge of the main panel and the seam allowance is up. Once again, run a straight stitch one-half inch inside these two edges. Fold the triangle assembly out. All seams on the top side should look neat and finished. This will be the outside surface of the bag.

C . Now fold the material in half across its width. Use a thin piece of wood as a guide to draw an arc (with chalk, pencil, or pen) from the head opening corner (be sure to use the corner cut back most severely — not the one that allows for the forward flap) down to the aft end of the folded edge.

D . Cut the material on this curved line.

II. Next apply a vinyl or an acrylic binding all around the perimeter of the cut material.

A . Fold the binding in half down its length.

B . Sandwich the raw edge of the fabric with this binding strip.

C . Sew it in place with a zigzag stitch, if available, so that half is on one side of the cover edge and half is on the other.

III. Common sense fasteners (some call them "twist lock") should be installed all along the curved back of the cover. Be sure to place one near each opening but allow space for lines and the stay at all three corners. Space the fasteners on roughly 10" centers between these corner ones.

A . The fasteners along the forward side will go in the flap so that it can overlap the opening.

B . The fasteners along the arc should close the bag inside edge to inside edge.

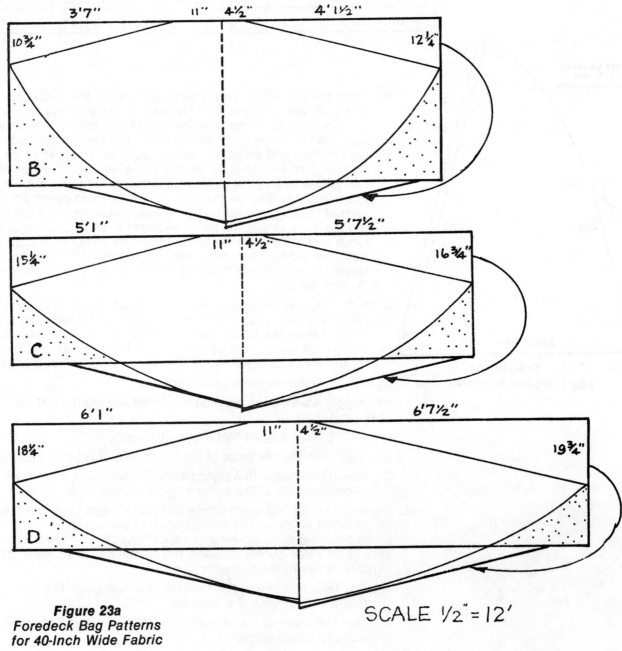

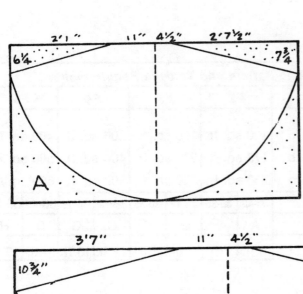

Figure 23a
*Foredeck Bag Patterns
for 40-Inch Wide Fabric*

SCALE ½" = 12'

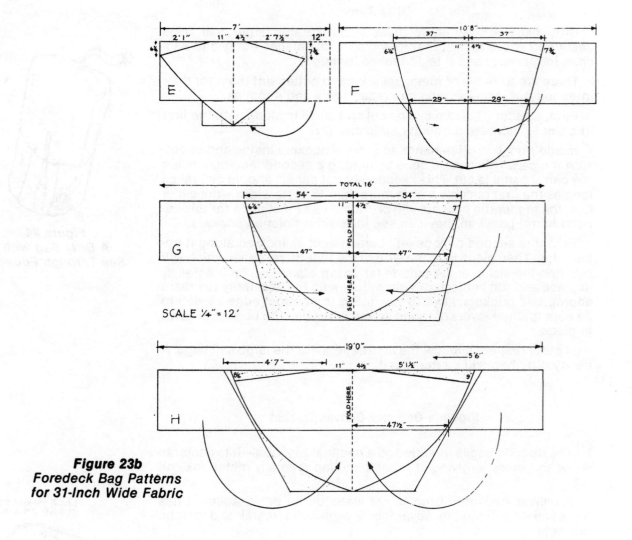

Figure 23b
*Foredeck Bag Patterns
for 31-Inch Wide Fabric*

IV. Between the fasteners on the arc side, sew mated strips of
Velcro tape so that the bag can be sealed quickly, if needed.
The Velcro should be roughly four inches long. Sew each tape
all around its edges with a straight stitch.

V. Sew nylon webbing handles approximately 12" long in place
along the center of the arc side. Use a "Box-×" stitch to hold
each end securely in place. The halyard can be fastened to
these handles if it is desired that the bag be lifted off the deck
to keep it dry and clean.

The cover is now complete. It can be used to store the sail
on deck or below. You may prefer to remove the cover completely when the sail is up or it can be left attached to the
forestay with the first common sense fastener only. However
this sail cover is used, it will be a favorite.

Ditty Bags

Ditty bags are generally made just like the larger sail bags described above except that they are much smaller—only 5 to 8 inches in diameter and 8 to 12 inches in height.

There are a couple of minor variations to better suit them for their intended purpose—storing sail repair tools and supplies.

First, a second bottom can be cut and sewn in along with the first in order to increase durability substantially.

In addition, it is often handy to provide pockets inside and/or outside the bag. This can be done by cutting a second rectangle when the barrel panel is cut. This "second barrel panel" should be just as long as the first but only a little more than ½ of its width—the wider it is, the higher the pockets will be. Some use Plastipane for this second barrel panel so they can see inside the finished pockets.

Hem this second or "pocket" barrel panel ½-inch all along it upper edge. Then place it on the side of the first barrel panel which will put it on the inside or the outside (at your preference). Pin it carefully in place and run vertical straight stitches up the assembly to create appropriate pockets. I like to sew along the bottom edge as well to be sure that the layers of fabric do not slip when the bottom is sewn in place.

In other respects, follow the instructions for the large sail bags. A handy ditty bag will be the result.

Figure 24
*A Ditty Bag with
See Through Pockets*

Rigger's Bag and Canvas Bucket

The rigger's bag is intended as a nautical tool box—it is easier to stow and more forgiving of rough handling than any metal box can be.

A canvas bucket is used to get water up on deck. Again, it has stowage and handling advantages over solid metal and plastic buckets.

These bags are essentailly large sail bags roughly 12 inches in diameter and 15 inches in height. But both must hold their shape. As a result, they are usually fitted with a 1/8- or a 1/4-inch thick plywood bottom. Simply cut the circular wood reinforcement, sand its edges, and slip it down into the bag. To be sure that it stays there, use a few small boat nails all round the bottom of the bag. Pull the fabric bottom of the bag tight as you tack the wooden bottom in place.

A further modification to produce improved shape retention is the installation of a boltrope all round the top of the bag. Hem the top of the bag without a drawstring. Then cut a length of 1/4- or 5/16-inch 3 strand rope 6 or 7 inches longer than the circumference of the bag opening.

With the bag on your knees—bottom away from you, pick up the upper side of the top of the bag. Lay the boltrope just in back of this edge. There should be 6 inches or so of rope to your left. The rest should be on the right. Now penetrate the bag rim about 3/16-inch below its edge. Then pass the needle round one strand of the rope just behind. Bring the needle over the top of the bag rim and penetrate it in the same way just over the next strand to the right in

LACE HANDLES TOGETHER

LEAD SINKER

Figure 25
A Canvas Bucket

the rope. Proceed all the way round the bag top in this manner. But stop when you are within 6 inches or so of the beginning point.

At this point unlay the rope ends and splice them together. Take two or three tucks and cut away excess rope. Now finish your boltrope stitch so the rim is neatly finished with a continuous ring of rope.

Grommets can be installed just under this roped edge. I prefer two rope handles in a rigger's bag. Space two No. 2 grommets about 4 inches apart on opposite sides of the bag. Then insert 9 or 10 inch 5/16-inch ropes into the holes from the outside. Knot the ends on the inside so they are locked in place.

The canvas bucket should be fitted with a long lanyard so it can be lowered to the water from the deck of the boat. Two grommets on opposite sides of the bag will provide for this. A rope sling about 1 foot long can be spliced from one to the other. Then a longer line can be snapped or spliced to this "handle."

Canvas buckets must tip on their side when they hit the water. To encourage this, you may want to sew a lead fishing sinker to one side of the bag.

12

Tote Bags

TOTE BAGS

Tote bags are, just as the title suggests, meant to carry clothing, food, and equipment. A "breathing" fabric should be used. Acrylics are most popular, but cotton, polyester, and nylon are also used. There are about as many styles and sizes as there are manufacturers. I am going to describe the construction of my favorite, but you should feel free to make modifications in size or design. The principles of construction will remain about the same.

The finished length of this bag will be 25½ inches and its diameter 11½ inches. Four pieces of cloth are required: a barrel, two end circles, and a pocket. These can be cut from a yard of 40-inch wide material, as shown in Figure 1 below. You will also need V-69 thread, 90 inches of 1½-inch or 2-inch nylon or polypropylene webbing, 27½ inches of #10 Delrin zipper, a zipper slide, and nine inches of ¾-inch wide Velcro tape.

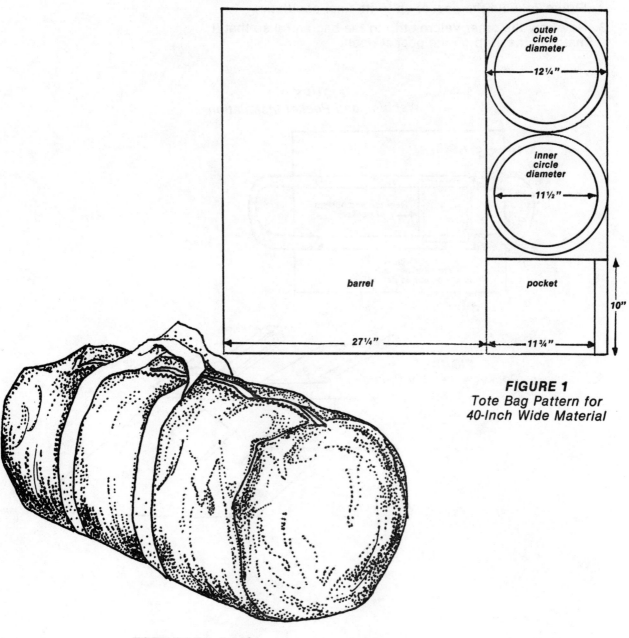

FIGURE 1
*Tote Bag Pattern for
40-Inch Wide Material*

To accurately form the circular end pieces, first cut two squares 12¼ inches on a side. Fold each in half and then fold again so that you are left with squares 6⅛ inches on a side. Use a short length of string and a pencil to form a makeshift compass and put down an arc from one "open" corner to the other. Cut along this arc. When the squares are unfolded, you should have two neat and accurate circles. The barrel of the bag and the pocket patch should also be cut from the fabric at this point.

Sew these parts together as directed below:

I. First prepare the barrel of the bag by installing the pocket rectangle. Its proper location is indicated in Figure 2.

   1. Fold one long edge of the pocket material as shown in Figure 3a. Sew this hem down and then sew one side of the Velcro strip in place over the hem as shown in Figure 3b.

   2. Sew the other long edge of the pocket in place as shown in Figure 3c. Fold the pocket up to its final position.

   3. Now sew the other Velcro strip to the bag barrel so that it matches the strip on the pocket itself.

FIGURE 2
Webbing and Pocket Installation

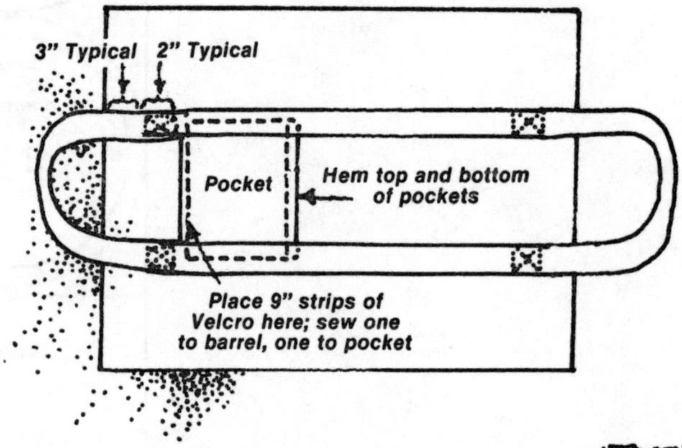

3" Typical   2" Typical

Pocket

Hem top and bottom of pockets

Place 9" strips of Velcro here; sew one to barrel, one to pocket

FIGURE 3
Pocket Assembly Detail

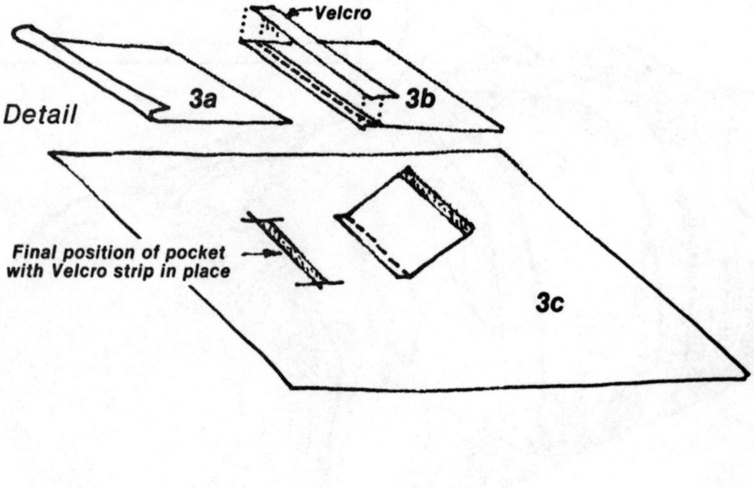

Velcro

3a   3b

Final position of pocket with Velcro strip in place

3c

II. Attach the webbing handle over the pocket

1. Sew the 90-inch length of webbing together forming a continuous loop.

2. Place marks on the webbing to indicate handle location. These marks should be three inches from the opening of the bag when sewn in place (as shown in Figure 2).

3. Sew the webbing to the material over the pocket ends, using a row of stitches along its edges. Either a straight or zigzag stitch may be used.

III. The zipper should be installed next.

1. Break the zipper in two and lay the tapes along the short sides of the barrel with the teeth inside and the cloth tape edge flush with that of the barrel. Sew both tapes in this

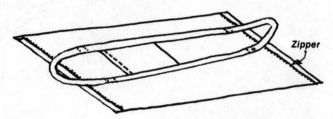

FIGURE 4
The First Step in Zipper Installation

position with straight stitches next to the zipper teeth (see Figure 4).

2. Put in a second row of stitches along both sides of the zipper tape after folding the seam allowance back along the barrel side of the seam, as illustrated in Figure 5. Leave a flap of cloth which covers the zipper teeth.

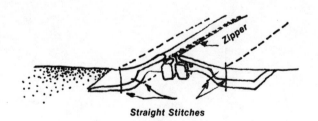

Straight Stitches

FIGURE 5
An End View of the Zipper Installation

3. Be sure to work the slide on so that the puller will be on the right side of the bag.

IV. Turn the bag so that it is inside out if it is not already so. Pin the two circular ends in place carefully and sew them with a row of straight stitches all around (see Figure 6).

V. Now you can turn the bag right side out. It is complete, though you may want to add a shoulder strap, end handle, or some other feature that will make the bag "just right" for you!

FIGURE 6
Bag Ends Pinned in Place Ready for Sewing

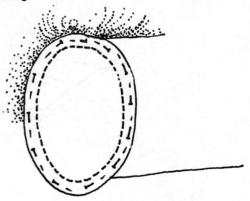

13

Sea Anchors

SEA ANCHORS

There are two types of sea anchors. One is intended to hold a boat relatively still in moderate weather. The other is intended to provide enough drag to slow a boat in a storm and keep it bow or stern to the wind and waves. The first type is often called a parachute anchor since it very closely resembles a parachute. The second is often called a storm anchor or a drogue. Both are useful to have on board and quite easy to make.

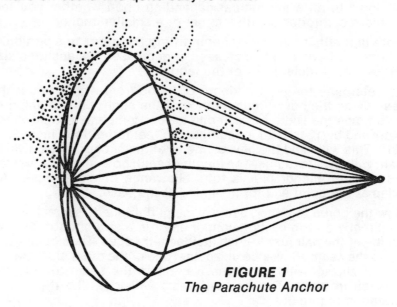

FIGURE 1
The Parachute Anchor

The Parachute Anchor

Parachute anchor (Figure 1) should be made of four-ounce nylon with the oxford finish. The nylon material is stronger and less expensive than Dacron. It is also much more durable than any natural fiber, like cotton or flax, in storage. Polyester thread (V-46) is appropriate. The only other materials needed will be grommets or rings, nylon webbing, and nylon line.

The size of a parachute anchor is not at all critical. Generally they are from 12 feet to 20 feet in diameter. The size of the boat, or rather its windage, should affect your decision as to the proper anchor size. There is, nevertheless, no "right" size. Just remember that the anchors become harder to store and to use as they increase in size.

This anchor is made up of wedge-shaped gores of fabric cut in accordance with the pattern in Figure 2. The base should be 59% of the width of the cloth that you are using. Half-way along their length, the gores should be 70% of their base. And three-quarters of their length from the base they should be 43% of that base width.

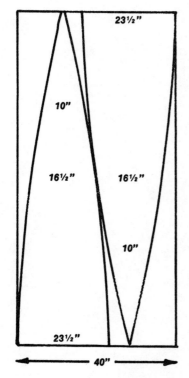

23½"

10"

16½"   16½"

10"

23½"

← 40" →

FIGURE 2
Parachute Anchor Gore Patterns

If a base of 23½ inches is used, it will be possible to cut two gores from each length of 40-inch wide cloth. To determine how many lengths of cloth will be required, follow the steps below:

1. Calculate the circumference of your anchor by multiplying its diameter by 3.1416 (pi).

2. Divide this circumference (in inches) by the base width of your gore panels less ½-inch for seams.

3. The result will seldom be a whole number but round up or down to an even number depending upon whether you feel more comfortable with a larger or a smaller anchor.

Note that rather than worry about fitting the gores to a particular diameter, we have simply increased or decreased the anchor's size to make most efficient use of the fabric.

To determine the proper length of fabric from which to cut the gores, divide the new circumference of the anchor (the number of panels times the width of each one less a ½-inch seam allowance and divided by 12 to reduce the figure to feet rather than inches) by 3.1416. This will yield the new diameter of the anchor. That, divided in half, will give its radius. The length of each gore should equal the radius of the anchor plus a total allowance of eight inches for overlap at the point and for hemming at the base.

Sew the gores together, using a "semi-flat felled" seam. Lay one gore directly on top of its neighbor and run a straight stitch down one side of the pair just ½-inch inside their edges. Then open them up, fold the seam allowance up against one or the other side and run a row of zigzag stitches all the way down the seam to hold the allowance in place. The finished seam will look like the one illustrated in Figure 3.

Proceed in this fashion until all of the gores are together forming a complete circle. Note that the final seam can be completed just like all of the others. The two panels can be placed on top of one another and sewn. Then the whole assembly can be turned inside out to open them up.

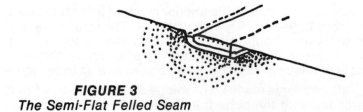

FIGURE 3
The Semi-Flat Felled Seam

Next cut out an opening in the center of the fabric assembly roughly one foot in diameter. This will permit water to flow over and through the anchor. That flow will stabilize the anchor—otherwise it would tend to oscillate back and forth.

Nylon webbing (from one to two inches in width) should be sewn over the seam allowance side of every other seam to provide a network of reinforcing ribs. Simply run two rows of straight stitches down each length of webbing—one along each edge.

Then use two-inch webbing folded in half along its length to reinforce and protect the fabric edge (Figure 4) at the hole in the center of the anchor and all around its outside. Once again, use two straight stitches to attach the webbing. The first should be just inside the folded edge and the second right along the open edges of the webbing.

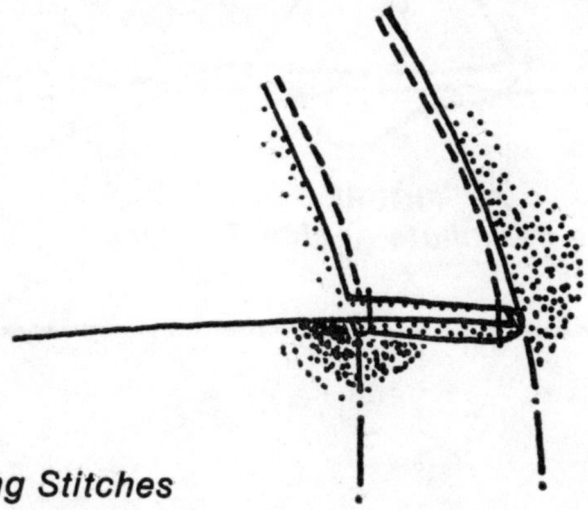

FIGURE 4
A Detail of Edge Webbing Stitches

The anchor shroud lines should be equal in length to the radius of the parachute (this is not critical—it is meant as a rough guide only). There should be one shroud line attached to each webbing rib radiating out from the center of the parachute. The other end of all the lines should be brought to a #3 or #4 stainless steel D-ring and tied securely to it. This, in its turn, can be hooked to a stout line between 50' and 150' long which will secure the anchor to the boat.

One major point remains to be considered: the manner in which the shroud lines are fastened to the parachute. No. 3 spur grommets placed over the rib webbing and the outer circumference webbing where the two intersect is satisfactory. But I prefer to use a six-inch to eight-inch loop of webbing which can be sewn carefully to the reinforcing webbing of the parachute (Figure 5), forming a loop to which the shrouds can be attached. Stitch all around the ends of the webbing loops and then across the diagonals of the rectangular box of stitches that results.

The parachute anchor is now ready to use. It will be found quite easy to deploy. There should be no need for weights or special bridles. Retrieving the anchor, however, may be somewhat difficult unless a trip line is tied to one grommet or webbing loop at the parachute's edge. This can then be used to make the anchor stream when it is hauled aboard.

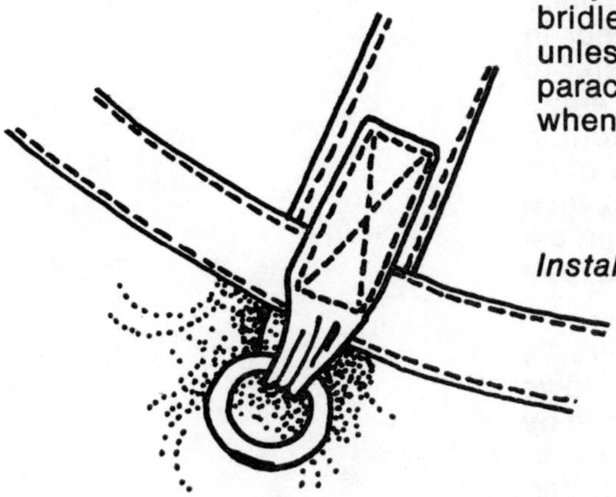

FIGURE 5
Installation of Shroud Line Rings

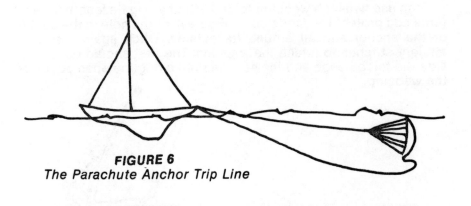

FIGURE 6
The Parachute Anchor Trip Line

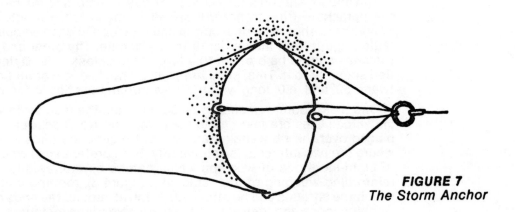

FIGURE 7
The Storm Anchor

The Storm Anchor

The storm anchor (Figure 7), too, can be made of four-ounce nylon oxford. Because of its size and the manner of its construction, there will be a little more stress on it than on the parachute anchor in spite of its intended use in severe storms. Even so, many prefer to move to a heavier eight-ounce nylon Cordura fabric or even eight-ounce Dacron sailcloth—it "seems" more appropriate. In addition to the fabric, you will require thread (V-69 or V-92, depending upon whether four-ounce or eight-ounce cloth is employed), 5/32-inch vinyl-coated wire rope (1 × 19, 7 × 7, or 7 × 19—the construction used is not critical), brass rings, a stainless ring, binding tape and rope to make up a bridle.

Begin your work with a circle of 5/32-inch vinyl-coated wire 24 inches in diameter (the wire should be 77 inches long—this allows for a 1½-inch overlap at the ends to form a circle). This circle can be completed by nicopressing a zinc-coated copper sleeve in place or it can be clamped with cable clamps. The Nicopress sleeve is certainly stronger, more compact and better looking, but the cable clamp can be installed easily and quickly with ordinary tools—it will be more than strong enough.

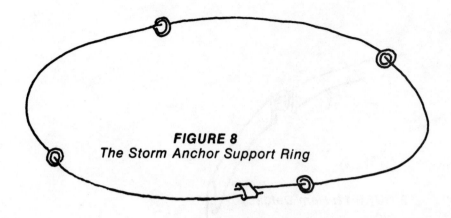

FIGURE 8
The Storm Anchor Support Ring

Before closing the circle, slide four 1¼-inch brass rings onto it. These will be used to rig a bridle securing the anchor to its line.

Then turn to the fabric that you will use. Cut from it two trapezoids as shown in Figure 9.

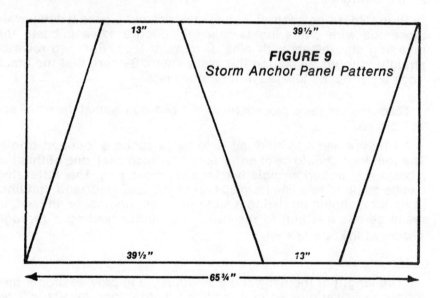

13"   39½"

FIGURE 9
Storm Anchor Panel Patterns

39½"   13"

◀———— 65¾" ————▶

FIGURE 10: *Ring Cutouts*

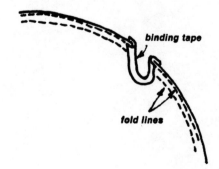

binding tape

fold lines

Lay one cloth trapezoid on top of the other so that all of their edges are flush. Secure them together with a row of straight stitches 5/8-inch inside each sloping edge. Then turn the assembly inside out to hide the seam allowance inside the anchor "sock." It is a good idea to fold this allowance up against one side or the other and sew it down with a row of zigzag stitches. That will increase the seam's strength and improve its appearance.

At four points spaced equally around the large end of the sleeve, cut away 2¼ inches deep by one inch wide rectangles of cloth to form openings for the brass rings in the hem to be fashioned next. Line these openings with binding (Figure 10) to protect them (use leather or prepared fabric binding). Simply fold the binding in half along its length, sandwich the raw fabric edge with it and sew it in place with a zigzag stitch.

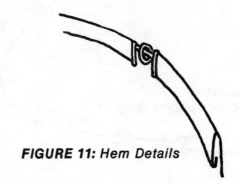

FIGURE 11: *Hem Details*

Fold ¼-inch of the cloth at the wide end of the sleeve to the inside of the sock all around the opening. Sew it down with a row of straight stitches.

Then fold inside another inch of material and crease it down well. Place the wire circle inside this fold (Figure 11) and baste the resulting sleeve/hem with pins or transfer tape. Run two rows of straight stitches all around this sleeve/hem. Be sure that the brass rings are properly located in their openings.

Following the same procedure, form a one-inch hem at the small end of the sock.

All that remains to be done is to tie or splice a four-part bridle. The four legs should be of equal length. Attach each one of them to a brass ring and to a single two-inch stainless ring. This latter ring can be secured to a line from 50 feet to 200 feet long* and that line, in its turn, should be tied to a stout cleat on the boat or, indeed, in really severe weather, to the mast itself (after leading it through chocks at the bow or stern.)

---

*The length of the line should be adjusted to provide proper performance in various water conditions. Large, long swells will require more line than small, short ones.

14
Weather Cloths and Hatch Covers

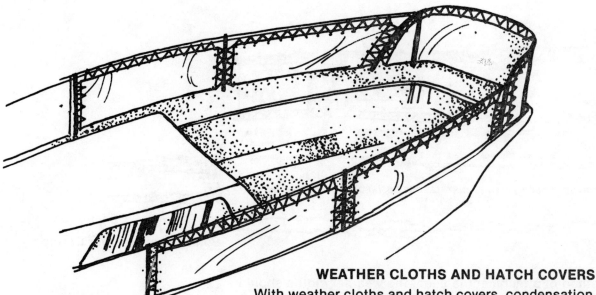

FIGURE 1
*Laced Weather Cloths
on a Sailboat*

WEATHER CLOTHS AND HATCH COVERS

With weather cloths and hatch covers, condensation is not likely to be a problem. Durability in sunlight, wind and water resistance are the prime requisites of fabric used for these items. Thus, polyester, vinyl-coated polyester, and acrylic materials are all appropriate. Additional materials needed are thread, fasteners, and perhaps tie line.

Weather Cloths

I want to consider weather cloths (some call them "spray dodgers") first. These are fabric pieces fastened into the life lines to provide temporary bulwarks which protect those in the cockpit from wind and spray. They are essentially nothing more than rectangular sections with hems all around. In some cases, especially in the way of stern pulpits, shaping will be required to provide a proper fit. But, even there, little difficulty is likely to be experienced. The problems encountered with weather cloths have to do with securing them in place, and I will devote the bulk of my attention to that. Sizes and construction details will depend upon the method of attachment in any case.

Whatever method you select, it should accomplish two things. First, it should secure the weather cloths adequately—that means that they must withstand breaking waves and howling winds. Second, it must make their putting up and taking down quick and convenient. There are three methods that I have found particularly successful in meeting these requirements.

Lacing. The first of these, lacing, is probably far and away the most commonly used (see Figures 1 and 2). It entails nothing more than spacing grommets every eight inches or so all around the weather cloths in a hem finished to one inch. These, then, are used to thread a small line (I like #505 Dacron leech line or ¼ inch 3-strand Dacron line) round stanchions and life lines in a continuous zigzag pattern that is quite attractive. For really serious cruising, it is a good idea to install screw eyes along the rail if there are otherwise no attachment points there. Then the fabric can be laced along its bottom as well as at its end and top. Or you may prefer using common sense surface-to-cloth fasteners along the outside edge of the toe rail. A separate panel can be run continuously over several stanchions so long as there is little curvature to the deck. If the deck curves, you will need to seam the panel in order to make its run correspond to that of the deck (wedges of material must be cut away.)

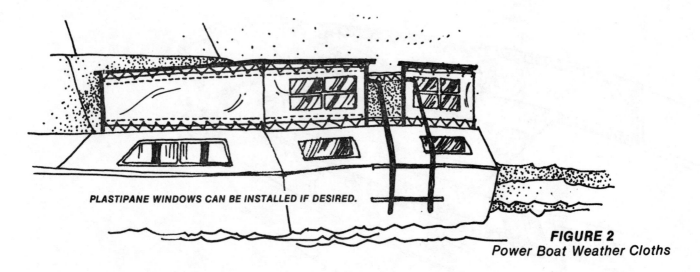

PLASTIPANE WINDOWS CAN BE INSTALLED IF DESIRED.

FIGURE 2
Power Boat Weather Cloths

If this method of attachment is used, the weather cloths should be from two to six inches less in height than the life line to which they will be laced. That will provide a gap from one to three inches wide at the top and the bottom which will enable the lacing to properly stretch the fabric. Be sure to allow an extra 1½ inch of cloth on all sides for hems. Sew the hems carefully in place before installing the grommets. Fold over first 1/2 inch of cloth, then fold again to form a one-inch finished hem. Staple or pin the hems in place carefully before sewing. Corners can be right angles or slightly truncated, whichever you prefer.

This method of attachment is certainly the most secure of the three presented here, but it is also the slowest to rig and unrig. This presents a special difficulty if a way is needed to board the boat frequently through the life lines. You may want to select one of the methods below if a boarding entrance is desired — either for the entire boat or for the entrance only.

Buttons. The button system (see Figure 2) makes weather cloth put up and take down extremely fast, but it gives up in security what is gained in convenience. It is nothing more than several wooden buttons sewn on a line run all around each weather cloth. These can then be looped round a life line or stanchion and merely buttoned into the line.

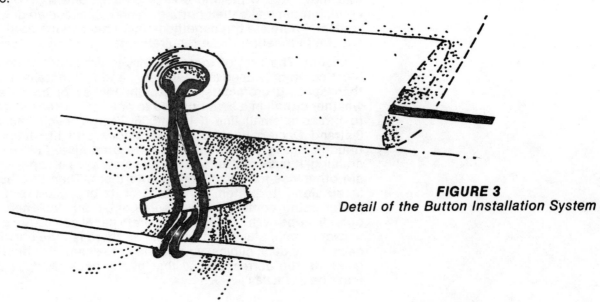

FIGURE 3
Detail of the Button Installation System

Just as in the case of the laced cloths, build these from three to six inches narrower than the height of the lifelines above the deck so that there will be a gap at the top (and, if desired, the bottom). These cloths can also be either continuous over one or more stanchions or they can be built so there is a separate panel for each pair of stanchions. Be sure to cut all panels to allow for 1½ inches of extra cloth for hems on all sides.

Fold over 1/2 inch of this allowance on all four edges of each panel. Crease the fold well so that you can easily see it. Then install #2 spur grommets in the middle of the remaining one inch of hem allowance (be sure to install the grommets with the 1/2-inch flap down so that the grommet penetrates two layers of cloth over half of its area). Begin by placing two grommets on either side of each corner—their center should be exactly four inches from the corner. Evenly space additional grommets between these on roughly 12-inch centers.

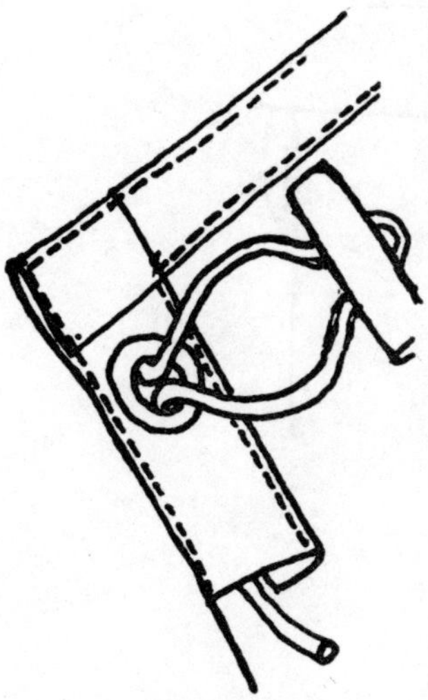

Now fold over the final one inch of excess cloth all around each panel. Staple or pin these hems in place carefully. Place a row of straight stitches just inside the folded edge. Then sew all around the inside edges of the hems with a second straight stitch. This will leave an open sleeve all around the panels through which a small braided line can be worked.

Note that there must be a grommet placed very close to the corner in order to keep it from curling when the line is pulled tight (see Figure 4).

FIGURE 4
Detail of the Corner Hem in a Buttoned System

Tie the line (I like to use #505 leech line here) to a small length of clothes hanger bent straight with rounded ends and work it all around the fabric through the hem. But fish the line out at each grommet and slip on a dowel "button." Pull out at least five inches of bight. The buttons should be roughly 1/2 inch by 2½ inch. Drill holes in their centers just large enough for the line that you are using. The line should eventually be brought out through the same grommet into which it was initially inserted (usually a lower corner grommet). Only when this point is reached can you cut the line from its source spool, leaving at least seven inches of excess line on both tails at the entry/exit grommet. Leave the two tails at this entry/exit grommet without a button.

That is all there is to it. The buttons can be taken around life lines, stanchions, deck fittings, etc., and threaded through the two lines exiting the grommets in the fabric. Buttons not opposite a good attachment point can simply be ignored. When all are in place, pull the two lines at the entry/exit grommet tight and secure them around a stanchion base.

Fasteners. Snap fasteners or common sense fasteners can be used for weather cloths if maximum protection from the elements is desired (there will be no gaps between the cloths and the deck or the lifelines). The fasteners also make put up and take down quick and easy. Their major problem is strength — they can come undone at just the wrong times.

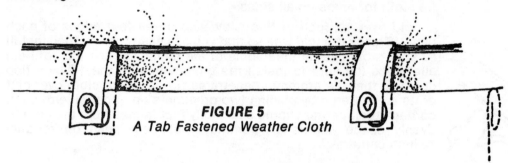

FIGURE 5
A Tab Fastened Weather Cloth

To maximize their strength, make every effort to keep loading in shear instead of peel. This is accomplished along the top of the weather cloths by fashioning a flap of cloth (or a series of tabs) that goes over the lifeline and fastens back on itself. Along the bottom, secure the fabric along the inside or the outside of the toe rail. I prefer to lace the ends of snapped panels since there is no good way to keep loading in shear on the fasteners there and, in any case, the lacing will insure that the cloths will stay in place even if the snaps come undone.

Start with the height of the lifelines above the deck. Allow the normal 1½-inch hem all around snapped cloths, as well as an additional two inches in width to provide for the flap at the top. If that two inches of extra cloth means that a good portion of the width of cloth off the bolt will be wasted, simply substitute four-inch by one-inch tabs on 3/8-inch centers for the flap. Once again, length will depend upon whether a panel is desired for each stanchion pair or for several stanchions.

Space the fasteners on roughly eight-inch centers. At corners, you may want to place to fasteners very close together for increased strength. Salt water will make all but the best ones completely useless in less than two months. Even the best fasteners will require replacement every two or three years.

Deck Hatch Covers

Hatch covers serve two purposes: they help prevent leaks through hull openings, and they protect varnished or oiled wood from the sun.

They are very easy to make. If the hatch is less than 3 inches above the deck, simply cut a piece of fabric to fit the hatch, allowing 1½ inches for hems and enough additional cloth to extend down the sides of the hatch frame to the deck forming a "skirt."

Fold the corners of the cloth blank to provide the proper skirt (remember to add the 1½-inch hem allowance to the necessary skirt length). Begin by placing the outside of the fabric (if your fabric has a right and a wrong side) down over the hatch. Crease the fabric along the edges of the hatch top to clearly outline it. Now fold the cloth in the margins together at the corners and sew them carefully together. Turn the cover right side out and fit it in place. If the fit is not snug and trim, make adjustments.

FIGURE 6
A Low Hatch Cover "Wrong Side Out"
with Pinched Corners

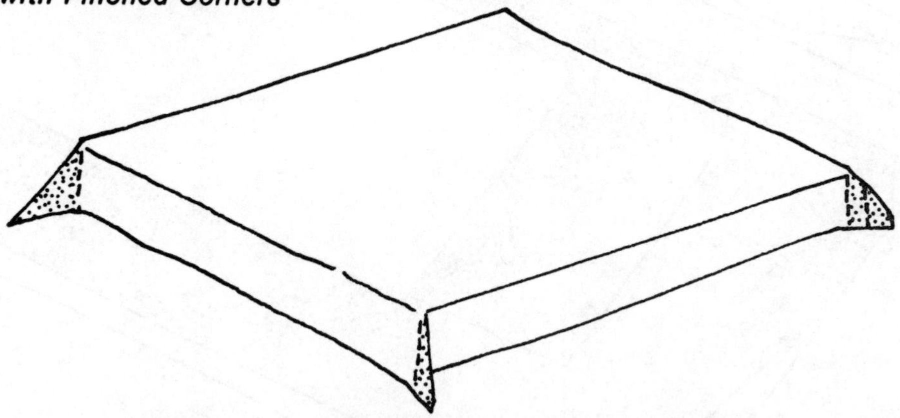

trim back to dashed
line, leaving ½-inch
seam allowance

Next, fold under the 1½-inch hem allowance all round the cover and sew it in place after first creasing it well to provide a clear sewing guide. There will be less chance for error if your first line of stitches is located within 1/8 inch of the creased edge. A second row of stitches can then be installed along the inside edge of the hem.

Locate snap fasteners or common sense fasteners or Velcro strips at the corners of the cover and on roughly 24-inch centers along each edge. With smaller covers, a single fastener in the center of each side will be sufficient. Install the fasteners first on the surface of the boat and then mark the proper point for their installation in the fabric to assure proper mating.

Greenhouse hatches and all others that have a height greater than 3-inches should be covered with an assembly of cloth panels. Each panel should be shaped to fit one face or facet of the protruding hatch. All should be cut with a ½-inch seam allowance wherever they will be sewn to other panels, and with a 1½-inch allowance wherever a hem will be required to provide a finished edge. All sewing should be done by placing the outside surface of one panel against the outside surface of its neighbor. Then a row of straight stitches should be run just ½-inch inside the edges to be joined. When the assembly is turned right side out, all seam allowances will then be inside. Follow the procedure outlined for the flatter hatch covers above to finish an "assembled" hatch cover along its deck edge.

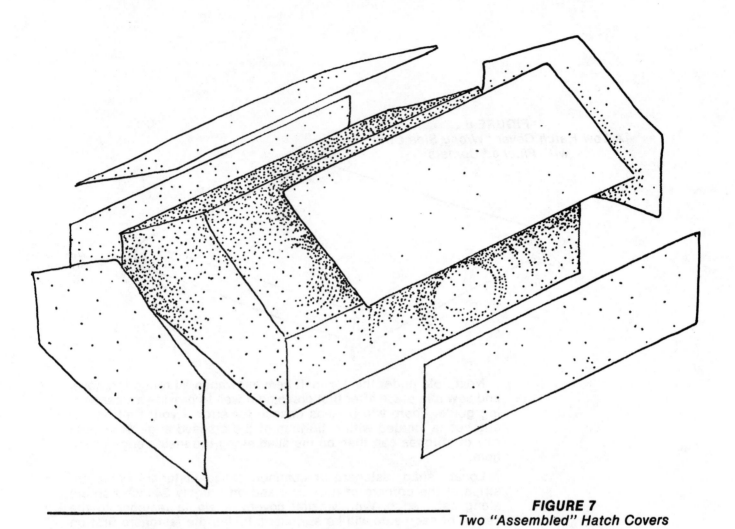

FIGURE 7
Two "Assembled" Hatch Covers

Boot for winches (typical)

Mast collar, sewn to panels 1, 2, and 3

Cut some "round" in this edge so cover fits deck contour

Let this edge overlap matching edge on panel "1"— The edges may be secured with Velcro

Align this edge with chain plate

Stitch to cover   Grommet

Tie-line to stem

Shape panel to cover teak hatch drops and trim

Tie-line to chain plate

From the Santana 20 Newsletter
Another "Assembled" Hatch Cover

Tie-line to genoa fairlead or to stanchion base

Windcatchers

15

WINDCATCHERS

There are an infinite number of windcatcher designs possible. Most of them will perform very well—providing additional ventilation in hot and muggy weather. I want to describe a design here that was conceived by Tisha Whitney (see the April, 1979, issue of *Cruising World*). We have made some minor changes in Tisha's original version, but the idea is hers. This catcher has two distinguishing features—it is effective no matter which direction the wind blows (making continual shifts of "set" unnecessary) and it can be "reefed" under a tent cover so that, even in a storm, fresh air can be funneled below without accompanying rain.

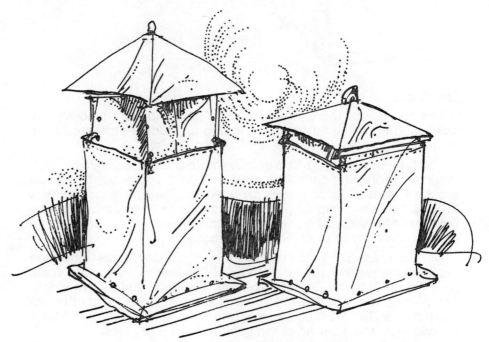

FIGURE 1: *The Windcatcher Shown Snapped at Different Heights*

The catcher (see Figure 1) is comprised of three sections: the waterproof funnel that is secured to the outside of a hatch, the waterproof tent top with "eaves" to provide rain protection, and an "X" shaped inner sail to catch the wind and direct it below. The sail is secured to the funnel with snaps so that it can be raised and lowered—sending more or less air below.

I recommend a vinyl-coated polyester material for the funnel and the tent since it is perfectly waterproof. The sail can be made of a lightweight nylon (from 3/4 ounce to 1½ ounces in weight). Thread used should be polyester since it is so strong and durable. Other materials needed will be webbing (nylon, polypropylene, or polyester), some wooden or plastic "spreaders" or crossbars, snap fasteners, grommets, and some snap hooks.

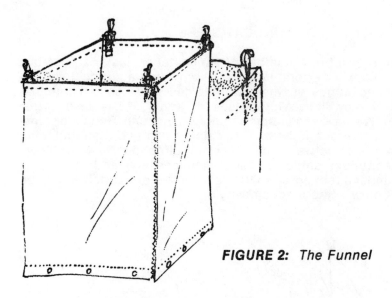

FIGURE 2: *The Funnel*

The Funnel

The purpose of the funnel is to raise the wind sail up above any obstruction like the hatch cover. It also provides a protected zone into which the sail can be lowered in order to reef it.

The funnel (see Figure 2) is nothing more than a rectangle of vinyl-laminated polyester cloth 31 inches wide and long enough to go all around the outside of the hatch opening. Thus, if your hatch is 25 × 20, the fabric should be 90 inches long to encircle it. Add one inch for seam allowance and one or two inches more so that the funnel will easily slide over the hatch flange.

As the seam allowance above indicates, there is just one side seam necessary for the fabrication of the funnel. Form this seam (see Figure 3) by folding the material face-to-face along its length and placing a row of straight stitches about 1/2 inch inside the two flush edges. The 1/2-inch seam allowance can then be folded back on one side and a zigzag stitch used to hold it in place.

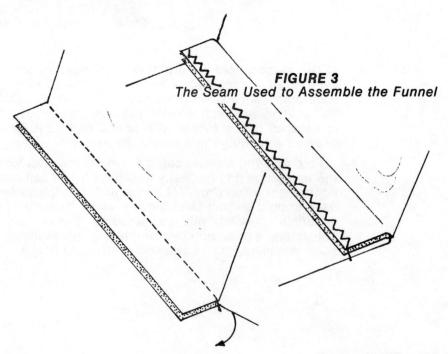

FIGURE 3
The Seam Used to Assemble the Funnel

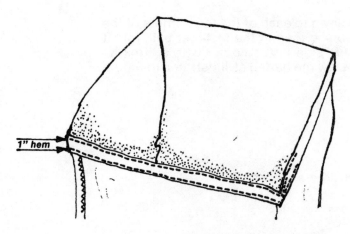

FIGURE 4: *Funnel*
Showing Hem and Corner Seam on Outside

Next form one-inch hems at the top and bottom of the funnel by folding the material back on itself (Figure 3). Make sure that the seam allowance for the side seam is on the outside at this point (the funnel will be inside out)(Figure 4). The hems, too, should be on the outside. Use two rows of straight stitches to secure the hems. Be sure to place the first row of stitches next to the folded edge. That will hold the fabric in place when you install the second row one inch or so further inside.

FIGURE 5: *Funnel*
Turned Right Side Out and Slit to Receive Battens

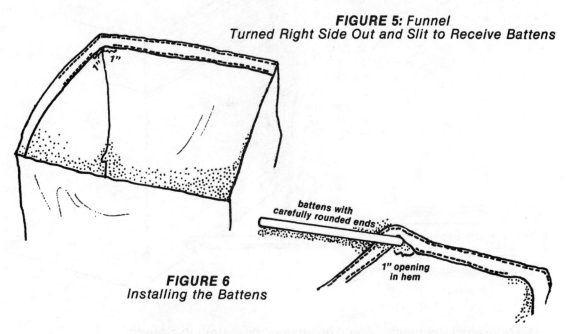

FIGURE 6
Installing the Battens

Turn the funnel right side out (Figure 5). Cut 5/8-inch plastic or wood battens to match all four sides of your hatch opening and rip the stitches along the upper hem for about one inch along each side of the funnel so the battens can be inserted (see Figure 6). When all four battens are in place, sew the hems shut again and sew across each corner also so they will be held in place along all four sides. These battens keep the funnel from collapsing in a breeze.

Snap fasteners can now be sewn to each of the top corners of the funnel. Insert a three-inch webbing loop in the fastener bail, fold it over and sew it in place on one side in the corner with a "Box X" stitch. All sewing should be below the batten as illustrated in Figure 7.

FIGURE 7
Snap Fasteners Attached at Corners

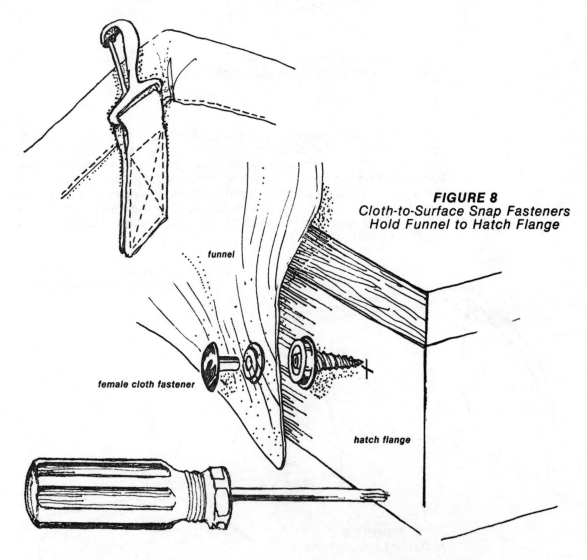

FIGURE 8
Cloth-to-Surface Snap Fasteners Hold Funnel to Hatch Flange

funnel

female cloth fastener

hatch flange

The bottom of the funnel should be finished by installing cloth-to-surface snap fasteners (see Figure 8). Match the female cloth fasteners with studs in the hatch flange so the funnel can be snapped securely in place. To install the studs you will need a Phillips screwdriver. Be careful to align the battened-opening of the funnel over the open hatch.

The Tent Top

The tent top (Figure 9) is a square or rectangle of vinyl-coated polyester fabric. It should be large enough to extend 8 to 10 inches beyond the funnel on all sides—this provides the protection necessary to keep rain out. Thus, for a hatch opening 25 x 20, you should cut the top 42 x 37—17 inches extra for eight-inch overhangs and 1/2-inch hems on both sides.

FIGURE 9: *The Finished Tent Top*

Sew these hems in place with two rows of straight stitches just as you did the hems at the top and bottom of the funnel. Then make up reinforced corner pockets. Cut four six-inch strips of two-inch wide webbing with a hotknife so they will not ravel. Fold them in half and sew down both sides with a row of straight stitches. Then stitch a pocket to each corner by running a second row of straight stitches down each side (Figure 10).

FIGURE 10: *Tent Top*

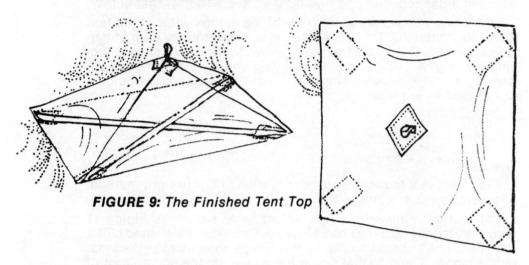

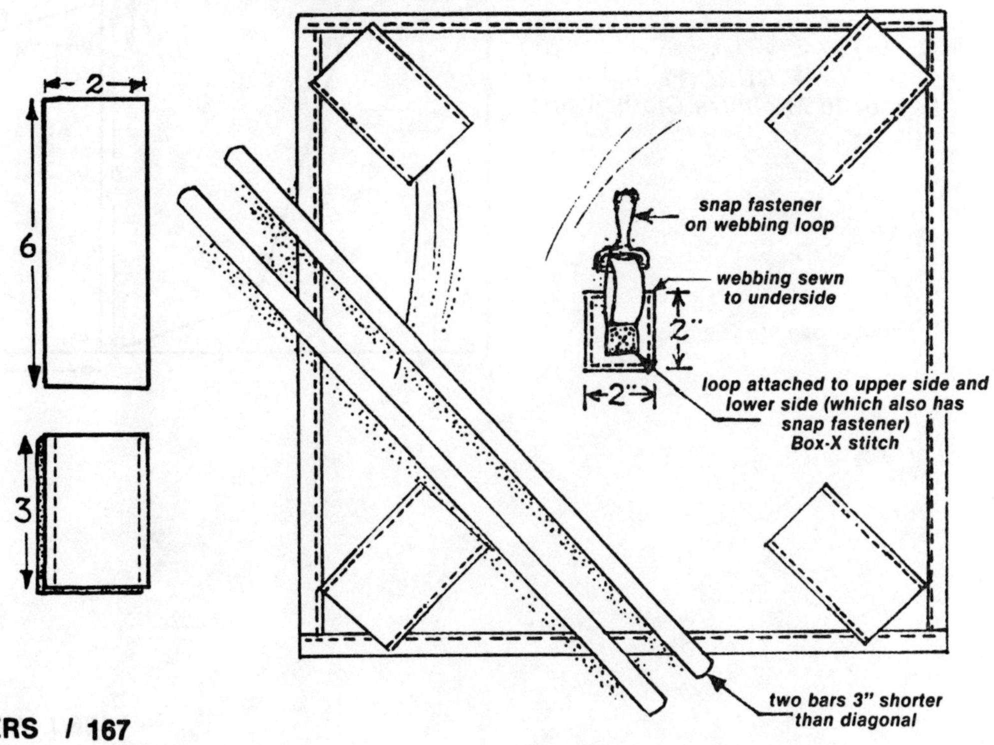

snap fastener
on webbing loop

webbing sewn
to underside

2"

2"

loop attached to upper side and
lower side (which also has
snap fastener)
Box-X stitch

two bars 3" shorter
than diagonal

These pockets will be used to contain cross bars. The bars can be PVC pipe or plastic or wooden sail batten material. Do carefully round the ends of whatever you use so it will cause as little chafe as possible. Make each bar about three inches shorter than the diagonal measurement of your tent top so there will be excess fabric to form the peak of the tent. You can figure the diagonal either by measuring the finished top or by adding the square of two adjacent sides together and finding the square root of that sum.

Sew a two-inch square piece of webbing in the center of the tent top to its underside. This should be used to reinforce a loop of narrower webbing (3/4 to one inch wide) sewn to the top to make a topping lift ring. A second loop of webbing can be used underneath (see Figure 10) to secure a snap hook—this will be used to hook the top of the sail in place.

The Sail

The "sail" is a crisscrossed construction of lightweight material designed to catch a breeze from any direction and funnel it below.

Cut four sail panels from lightweight nylon sail cloth. Figure 11 below illustrates how they can be laid out to minimize wasted cloth. Dimension "A" should be two inches longer than half the diagonal of the funnel. The diagonal of the funnel will be the square root of the sum of the squares of two adjacent sides. Or, if this is confusing, you can simply measure your funnel across the diagonal. Dimension "B" should be 1½ times that diagonal. Corner "c" should be a 90° angle. The peak height "F" should be 10 inches. Side "D" should be the width of the cloth (usually from 40 to 42 inches). Sides "C" and "E" will be determined by these other dimensions.

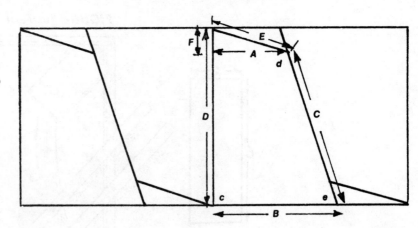

FIGURE 11
Layout to Minimize Cloth Waste

Fold over each edge of all four panels twice. The hems need be only 1/4-inch wide (Figure 12). Edge "C" should be reinforced with one-inch webbing along one side (Figure 13). Into this press #1 or #2 grommets. Start at corner "d" and install four grommets. They should be evenly spaced along the edge, but note that there is no grommet needed in corner "e."

FIGURE 12
Folded Edges for ¼-Inch Hems

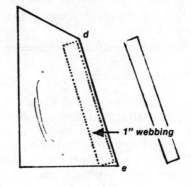

FIGURE 13
Webbing Reinforcement

FIGURE 14
Sleeves to Contain Crossbars

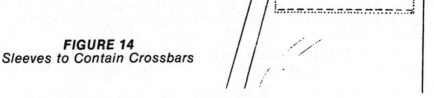

Using scraps of sail material, cut two-inch wide by 12- or 13-inch long rectangles. Sew these along their long edges across the top of each sail panel as shown in Figure 14. Note that the sail panels are matched up and the rectangles are sewn to the forward side of matched panels (Figure 15). The ends should be left open to form sleeves for the insertion of the cross bars to spread the tent top. The sleeves should be wide enough to permit the crossbars to cross one another.

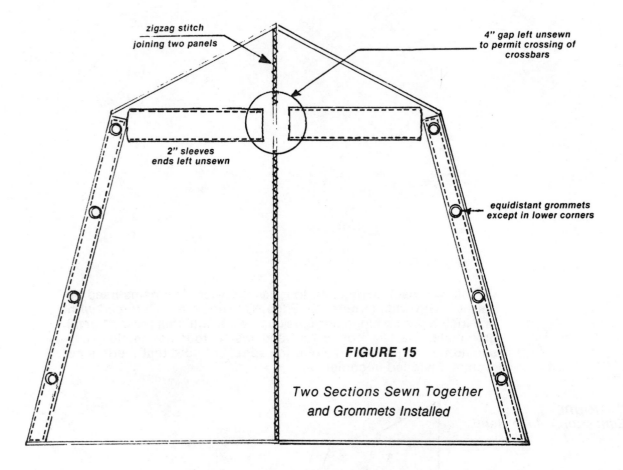

zigzag stitch
joining two panels

4" gap left unsewn
to permit crossing of
crossbars

2" sleeves
ends left unsewn

equidistant grommets
except in lower corners

FIGURE 15

*Two Sections Sewn Together
and Grommets Installed*

Now sew the paired sail panels together with a simple overlapping seam 1/2-inch or so wide. A single row of zigzag stitches will do very well here. Leave a four-inch opening in the way of the crossbar sleeves so the bars can cross over one another. These openings do not have to be cut back—just leave their edges unsewn. Then join the two panel assemblies together with a single row of straight stitches down their center. Once again, be sure to leave that four-inch area unsewn. The four sail panels now form an "X" when they are fanned out about the center seam. The sleeves for the cross bars should be on the same side of the fabric on quarter panels opposite one another.

The final task to complete the sail assembly is the attachment of a small brass ring, through a nylon webbing loop, to the top (see Figure 16).

Assembly

Snap the sail to the tent top, insert the cross bars, and snap all four funnel corners to the grommets at one level of the sail. Secure the funnel to the hatch flange and hoist the tent top with a halyard. Your windcatcher should work perfectly. To reef down simply snap the corners of the funnel to higher grommets.

If you need to store the catcher, it can be easily disassembled. Then it will roll into a very small bundle. There are many possible variations on this design. Don't hesitate to use your imagination.

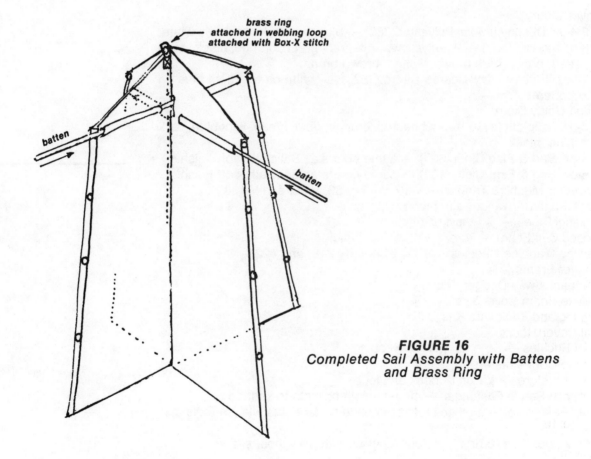

brass ring
attached in webbing loop
attached with Box-X stitch

batten

batten

FIGURE 16
*Completed Sail Assembly with Battens
and Brass Ring*

Jim Grant, the author of this book, is also the owner of Sailrite Kits, a mail-order company supplying sailmakers, amateur and professional alike, with quality fabrics and tools. Here is a listing of some of those products that are most useful for canvaswork. Too frequently, do-it-yourselfers are stymied by an inability to obtain the supplies they need. Every item mentioned in this book is available from Sailrite Kits. For current pricing and ordering, call toll free (800) 348-2769, or send $2.00 to Sailrite Kits, Route 1, Columbia City, IN 46725, for the Sailrite Sailmaker's Catalogue.

Cover Cloth
   8.4-oz. Destiny II Spun Polyester (36") — blue, brown, kelly green, white.
   8-oz. Acrylic (40") — blue, yellow, white, red, green, orange, black, deep dark brown, true brown, walnut, brown brun.
   12-oz. Weblon Vinyl-Coated Dacron (62") — white on top, light blue on bottom.
Nylon Utility Cloth
   4-oz. Sailcloth (41½") — white, red, orange, gold, green, light blue, dark blue, black.
   4-oz. Bag & Flag Cloth (60") — same colors as Sailcloth, soft finish.
   6-oz. Bag & Flag Cloth (46") — same colors as Sailcloth, soft finish.
Polyester Machine Thread — V-30, V-46, V-69, V-92, and V-138
Plasti-Pane (for windows in fabric panels)
Binding Tapes — ⅝" Vinyl or Acrylan
Closed Cell Foam — Airex, ½" to 2½" thick
Sewing Machine Needles — #11, #14, #16 , #18, and #22
Dodger Frame Kits
Companionway Dodger Kits
Deluxe Boom Cover Kits
Awning and Enclosure Kits
Sail Cover Hooks
Cam Buckles — ½", ¾", or 1" webbing
Lift-the-Dot Fasteners
Marine Velcro — ⅝" or 1" hook and loop
Common Sense Fasteners — cloth-to-cloth or cloth-to-surface
Snap Fasteners — cloth-to-cloth or cloth-to-surface. Installation tools also available.
YKK Zipper — #10 or #5, various lengths, with or without slider

Appendix